MW00962048

El Barrio

For Carmelita...... Ideas, Visions, Memories / Enjoy some visions The Latino-Experience the Experience Amirica

Humberto Pouero Vega

El Barrio

HUMBERTO CINTRON

Copyright © 2010 by Humberto Cintron.
Cover Illustration by Henry Rodríguez
Author photo taken by: George Malavé

Library of Congress Control Number: 2010912536
ISBN: Hardcover   978-1-4535-6408-0
               Softcover   978-1-4535-6407-3
               Ebook   978-1-4535-6384-7

All rights reserved. No part of this book may be reproduced or transmitted in any
form or by any means, electronic or mechanical, including photocopying, recording,
or by any information storage and retrieval system, without permission in writing
from the copyright owner.

This book was printed in the United States of America.

To order additional copies of this book, contact:
Xlibris Corporation
1-888-795-4274
www.Xlibris.com
Orders@Xlibris.com
71639

Introduction

When we look at work of a creative writer it is not enough to examine form, structure and content. The life of a writer offers us glimpses into their world and insights into the history of their time that formed and informed their work. Their experiences are the foundation upon which the writer builds his or her ideas. In Humberto Cintron we find a skilled wordsmith who intimately understands the impact of structure, the emotional nuances of storytelling and how to apply these literary dynamics to communicate the passionate intensity of his intended message.

Humberto Cintron was born March 9, 1936 in Metropolitan Hospital, on Welfare Island, in the middle of the East River where the 59th Street Bridge crosses into Queens. His parents arrived in New York City at least several years before that, and both his older brother, Roland, and his older sister, Milagros, were also born here. These are not just the words of a deeply intelligent being, but also the words of a second generation Puerto Rican whose family migrated to New York City in the early decades of the 20th century to confront the brutal challenges that awaited an entire wave of island immigrants. Some overcame these challenges, survived, thrived and moved onto greater self-realization and more fruitful lives. Some failed. And some learned how to adapt, to conquer obstacles on the ground of reality and build institutions that addressed the needs of the greater community.

In the midst of overwhelming cultural difficulties, Cintron finds jewels of creativity that keep his perseverance in tact. In his opening poem *Soul Puerto Rican* Humberto says about himself, " . . . The battle armor that I wear/Though dented, warped, and bled upon/Wears well with time . . ." He is full of faith in the possibility centered in his being and hope for the future, " . . . Once barren tree/ Alive with green . . . and reaching for the sun."

Cintron's takes us on a journey. The departure point is 1969 at a rally in the middle of Madison Avenue and East 111th Street, spearheaded by members of the Young Lords, a militant group of proud and empowered Puerto Rican youth. Surrounding them in *El Barrio '69* there are real people who represent the typical characters of the neighborhood. One by one Cintron introduces them to us in brief portraits. A politician, a tiny brown woman, a priest, a hustling entrepreneur, a political nun, a handsome young man, the addict, " . . . each one a universe unto himself . . . with dimensions beyond the façade . . ." He brings to light the essence of his world, and it is here, in *El Barrio*, otherwise know as East Harlem, New York City, where Humberto Cintron's world is revealed.

Tar Beach was the metaphor given to rooftop playgrounds where young Puerto Ricans went to fly their kites. *Tar Beach* was also the quiet haven for solitude, away from large families and crowed apartments, where Cintron would go to write. He paints the landscape of *Tar Beach* for us, "A blue toro with a long tail and twin orange diamonds sailed . . ." where a parade of colorful kites began flying from rooftops at dawn. It is in *Tar Beach* where we meet Bacalao, legendary kite master—and kite bully, skilled in the competitive sport of kite flight, determined to cut down all other kites in his territory.

This war story of kites becomes a reflection of the macrocosm. Cintron shares with us a profound realization, that all " . . . the empty space spread around and above me . . ." reminds him of his " . . . insignificance in the great scheme of the universe . . . ." We sense the significance of these acts of triumph and defeat found in Cintron's unique vista and in a future where " . . . tomorrow's television culture would change the rooftop landscape and drive kite flying into oblivion . . ."

In *The Artist* Cintron challenges stereotypical misconceptions " . . . of bearded eccentrics, super-sophisticates . . . and long-haired, sandal-and-faded-jean-wearing cavorters . . ." all creative, yet diverse individuals grouped into the one label—*artist*. He wants to know how these attitudes and ideas impact the average Puerto Rican, underlying an urgent awareness at a sociopolitical level as well. He is searching for the common denominator in " . . . the indomitable spirit of expression . . . ." within " . . . the reality of our present . . . ." Here, Cintron investigates his own creative directive in a " . . . responsibility of choices, transmitting to the observer . . ." Through his work Cintron reflects on the images of identity to uncover their deeper meanings.

In *La Pompa*, as in *Tar Beach*, Cintron paints a visual landscape with the eye of an artist. The view this time descends from the rooftops and explodes into the vibrant doings of a typical El Barrio neighborhood in the middle August on " . . . a hot, sticky, muggy New York summer day in 1944 . . . ." Cintron demonstrates his literary versatility in *La Pompa*, the name commonly given to the fire hydrant, otherwise known as the pump or the Johnny pump and explores voice through the other, namely, an inanimate object with the ability to think, feel and react like a human being. He draws us intriguingly into the movement of this story where we learn about "stickball" and "stoopball," a version of " . . . baseball played without a bat . . ." when the only playground available is the street.

In contrasts to the colorful, light-hearted depictions of community life found in *Tar Beach* and *La Pompa*, Cintron's writing takes a more serious turn. In *Otto Lived* and *Otto Died* Cintron recaptures tender sympathies for Otto, his friend, whose life was cut short by Otto's untimely death before his thirty-second birthday from the subsequent ravages of teen drug use. Cintron describes his friend's addiction and how " . . . his mind and life were out of his control and wasted on useless and meaningless pursuits on the streets . . . in the jail cells . . . and, finally, on a hospital bed in East Harlem . . . ."

Cintron is not only disheartened, but also angry at the system that exploits the addict, as well as the pusher who he describes as " . . . a vile, contemptible villain . . ." His condemnation stretches even further as he connects the dots and makes parallels " . . . about providers of non-substance . . ." who have " . . . similar, if not graver, effects on people . . . who saturate other people's minds with junk . . . ."; namely, television.

Like a skilled litigator he provides us with facts and statistics to support his case:

> "... a typical week of Spanish language television ... provides 12.5 hours of news; 3 hours of public affairs programming; 8 hours of sports; 2 hours of culturally oriented programming ... and 105 hours of 'entertainment programming' ... devoted to a mélange of situation comedies, variety shows, cartoons, old movies and ... soap operas, interspersed continuously and callously with an inordinate number of poorly produced commercials."

He makes comparisons between substance and technological addictions. His anger for the loss of his friend extends to advocacy on behalf of his community. Addiction exists in many forms. Cintron challenges the producers of Spanish language television to " ... assume responsibility for sharing in the education and the economic and social development of that market ..." and change " ... the mind pollution that rides the public airwaves today . . . ."

In the same way that conditioning and family values inform the growth and character of individuals, so does the element of *place*. Young students in a creative writing workshop write vastly different poems when they are in open spaces than they do inside the tight confines of a crowded classroom. Cintron often withdrew to the quiet solitude of the rooftop in order to hear his thoughts and, perhaps, to give them room to fly.

In many ways we become our surroundings. The essence of our neighborhood filters in and somehow manages to become part of our unique core. There is an interchange between person and place. But it is not just a one-way exchange. We do not just receive and accept the impact of what exists around us; we can also affect our surroundings destructively or creatively. Humberto Cintron is observing his neighborhood and taking notes. He allows the sound, timber, mood and flavor of his barrio to filter into his being and emerge through his consciousness translated into these stories, essays, poems and plays.

In *Across Third Avenue: Freedom* Cintron reaches a boundary of limitations that confronted every Puerto Rican immigrant, citizen and visitor at the time. Part of this boundary was defined by the Third Avenue El, " . . . a great, black, spiderlike iron monster . . ." that " . . . cast a checkerboard shadow, alternating with shafts of sunlight . . ." *El* is short for the elevated train that once ran north to south through El Barrio on Third Avenue and into the Bronx. He remembers at eight years old " . . . sitting on the curb, staring across to the east side of the street, the ominous, foreboding presence of the El weighing on (his) mind . . ." Beyond was another world, the Italian neighborhood " . . . complete with Ferris wheel, merry-go-round, pizza pies . . . fishing piers that extended into the East River and the Boys Club . . . ."

By 1955 service on the Third Avenue El was discontinued and during the 1960s it was dismantled due to rising protests of men in the real-estate business who considered the El to constitutes a menace to property values. But for Cintron, this invisible barrier was " . . . inside (his) head . . . Puerto Ricans were not to cross third avenue; that was Italian territory. Period . . . ." Reminiscent of the conflicts portrayed in the Broadway play and blockbuster movie *West Side Story*, the other side was strictly taboo, " . . . Beyond third avenue, you risked your life . . . ."

The barrier of the El over the years may have disappeared, but " . . . remnants . . . still linger . . . The wall of unwelcome still survives . . ." Yet, despite these barriers, Cintron states, "I never grew up bitter . . . ." Nurtured on communal values and family traditions, there was no end to the list of community services Cintron was enlisted to provide. He also grew up " . . . knowing that cruelty and violence and deceit were all part of the personal repertoire of social tools . . ." in the dichotomy of ethics that defined Cintron's early consciousness.

For Cintron the Third Avenue El became a subtext in his consciousness that followed him through the military, college, freedom marches in Mississippi, rent strikes, community action and antipoverty programs, experimental school districts, and rejections slips from publishers. And that still exists in every form of mass-communication media that

" . . . chooses to ignore the Puerto Rican editorially or carefully
selects the images it presents, thus helping to perpetuate
stereotypical negativism or promote a token Puerto Rican
personality . . . denying employment and opportunities to Puerto
Ricans exclusive of the mail room . . ."

Cintron brings a clear message of hope and determination, even though
he'll " . . . always sit on the curb somewhere, staring in the Third avenues
of the world . . . ." Cintron has learned his lessons. His consciousness has
matured from passive spectator into proactive participant. And it is here
we see that Cintron does cross the street to the other side and transforms
from victim—to survivor, marking a turning point to freedom.

Borinquen's Barrio Boys is a poem that captures a young boy's life on any
given day, " . . . Running, jumping, laughing, talking, in a . . . morning
reunion dance . . . ." We are invited into this world, not unlike the Lost
Boys in Peter Pan's Neverland, " . . . electrifying the morning and starting
the invasion of back lots, which each one knows like his own soul . . .
lithe, agile bodies climb breathtakingly, only to leap down on the other
side . . . swinging from fire escapes, past bedroom windows onto adjoining
buildings . . ." It is this figurative language that characterizes Cintron's
unique wit and writing style where we are transported back through time
as first-class passengers on this journey.

Humberto Cintron offers us an expanded view of the complex Puerto
Rican persona inherited from a sun-infused island culture. There are
some who do not understand what comes naturally to an animated
community that finds joy in camaraderie and fellowship. There are some
who cannot fathom why our community parks their beach chairs in front
of their apartment buildings during summer evenings to socialize with
each other. They don't understand the refreshing relief that brings people
outside to cool off in the evening after a scorching tropical day; behavior
that is uncharacteristic to those cultures from colder climates. It is these
specific cultural nuances that Cintron taps into to share with the reader.
There is nothing barbaric, offensive or inappropriate about these common,
communal rituals. It is the island way. Not just for Puerto Ricans, but also

for Cubans, West Indians, Dominicans, Mexicans and Africans among the many other cultures that evolved in tropical climates.

There are numerous gems to be found here in *El Barrio*, like *La Canción Del Asopao* that tributes the delectable palate of Puerto Rican cuisine. These stories, poems, essays and plays are treasures to be uncovered. They are not the stereotypically negative portrayals of Puerto Ricans that have shadowed us for centuries, but diamonds crystallized from the roughage of poverty, hunger and large families joined by communal determination not only to survive, but also to flourish.

Sandra María Esteves

Contents

Selected Works

By

Humberto Cintron

Acknowledgments

So many people to thank: Maria Laviera Cintron (Mom)—She taught us to love, to care and to share; Norberto Solis Cintron (Pop)—He shared the three Ds: decision, determination and dedication; Rolando Cintron, *The Song of Roland*—He opened the path and led the way. Mildred Cintron Cooper—Steady, solid, secure . . . sister. Otto Rosario—He created *The Dream* . . . but never lived it. Jack Agueros—Lifelong friend. We shared and lived . . . *The Dream*. Raquel Torres Cintron—First love—fourteen to sixty-eight;; Gloria Quinones, "I want to help my people."—An inspiration that fulfills dreams; Mr. Lavin, P.S. 83—"You can do it . . . It all starts here."; Mr. Mockler, P.S. 83—"Why not?"; Mrs. Eiter, P.S. 107—My first lesson. "Thank you, Mrs. Eiter!"; Luz Rodriguez—She closed the book!

Soul Puerto Rican

The day
is grey
ofay
But I've got sunshine up my sleeve
I've got a smile
No idle grin
I'll make another day begin

Depressed? Obsessed?
My music is a soul caressed;
And every day of strife I live
Rewards my heart with strength to give
The *battle* armor that I wear
Though dented, warped, and bled upon
Wears well with time
And nimble wit and laughter
Give resilience
To the agonized, tormented mind
I carry with me all the time

Tomorrow brings a fleeting thought
A scent
A scene
A happening
A something new
Or even old
Awakening a surge of life
Like *springtime*
Bursting into bloom

Once barren tree
Alive with green
Outstretched and reaching for the *sun*

El Barrio 1969

The autumn day in El Barrio finds a lithe, brown-skinned youth addressing a rally of people in the middle of Madison Avenue and 111th Street. Traffic is backed up to the silk stockings district. "Right on!" shout his comrades in purple berets and surplus military fatigues, as he pours forth the rhetoric of revolution. His words bring tears, anguish and rage to the milling crowd surrounded by glaring, anxious cops in shiny blue helmets. His is the poetry of poverty, challenging the mighty bastions of capitalist America that has been built on the bedrock of greed, deceit and calumny. His audience is composed mainly of other youth. There are dozens of them—spirited and articulate—the now generation of New York City's militancy. They are profane, profound, proud and Puerto Rican. These are the Young Lords.

Less than a block away, a silver-haired, aging gentleman in a grey, silk suit stands in a rest area of the crowded market place. This is *La Marqueta*, where the populace comes to shop. The man is shaking hands, smiling gold-toothed greetings to shoppers of all ages, and handing out leaflets extolling the civic qualities of two candidates for local elected office: one is black, and the other is Puerto Rican. This is a political marriage of the latter, a nondescript lawyer with little experience, and the former, a Tammany Hall operative who has been virtually ineffectual over thirty years of public life. The lawyer's only distinction is that the man handing out the leaflets is another perpetual, political presence whose main malfunction seems to be to make appearances on behalf of the Puerto Rican community in an attempt at representation with few effective results.

Further away in another block, sitting at the window of her ground-floor apartment, viewing the action on the block while simultaneously carrying on a conversation with a local priest standing outside and keeping her vision across the environs after her brood of mischievous children, a young woman talks about how to make her block a better place to live. Her apartment is often the center of activity for the 'small town' of her block: with a population of 4,500. The railroad flat houses her family of five and occasional relatives and friends and serves as a social gathering place for the block association. It is a place always alive with talk, laughter, children, rum, coffee and music. Her rich, generous smile greets every visitor with the warmth and the emotion to dispel stereotypes of New York City as a cold, insensitive place. Two cats glide silently through the house—pets and playthings to the children by day and sentries and guardians against rats by night. She has taught the priest more about love, God and spirituality than all his years on the pulpit, and he has taught her about herself and her personal strengths—something she never knew she had. Together, they share a common bond; he had to leave the confines of the church, and she had to cast aside her psychological armor to do it.

Another few blocks away bring us to the entrepreneur extraordinaire: He buys and sells everything and anything; his specialty is cars. He loans money and manufactures candy. At over seventy years of age, he dyes his hair jet-black, dons a mohair suit and buys tender, young women for a night or an hour with the hundreds and thousands of dollars he turns over everyday in his various enterprises. He spent half of his life in jail for neatly disposing of a police officer who abused his woman, but he returned in his old age to continue his never-forgotten hustle in the jungle of trash and tenements. He works sixteen hours a day, everyday. Yet he has never held a job in his life. He won't tolerate criticism of the United States. According to him, "You can always make a buck here."

The tiny, brown woman has raised three generations of children, not all her own. She cooks, sews, prays and loves—some say, more than anyone, anywhere, anytime. The children she has loved, taught and reared have shared her living example from the back lots of El Barrio to the board rooms and commissions of the local government. Her rice and beans are the subject of conversation in international circles, although she herself has seldom left her block for the past thirty-five years, except to shop or go to church.

There is a diminutive nun whose political views lean toward Puerto Rican nationalism, only blocks away. She serves in a social work capacity with a community agency—helping without humiliating—and all the while enraged that people should be in such condition to beg alms from the imperialist Yankee. She is particularly incensed over the cynicism demonstrated by the society that extracts in pride what they provide in dollars and the grudging attitude that permeates the social institutions that claim to serve the poor. She writes and speaks in every available public forum, assailing the multitude of community-serving agencies that pour their resources into the middle class while ignoring the neediest and the poorest among us. She dreams of and works for an independent and sovereign nation of Puerto Rico and sneers at Puerto Ricans' feeble attempts at developing political power in the US.

Further on, there is a young man in his early thirties. He is young and handsome. He dresses in the latest fashions and spends his weekend evenings at the night clubs and dance halls of midtown Manhattan. He has worked his way up from delivery boy, at age eighteen, to his current position as manager of a jewelry manufacturing firm. He owns a home outside the neighborhood, changes his new car every year, and appears to have all the comforts of Middle America. He is of the pleasure generation. He acquires things—color TV, trail bike, season tickets to Jets football games, stereo music system, condominium vacation in the Caribbean, Playboy Club membership, and a variety of credit cards to add more items as they become fashionable. He is clean. The women love it. The men envy it. For business purposes, he is called Mr. Martin; in El Barrio, he is called Pupo. He stops by occasionally to visit his parents and say hello to the old crowd. Then he whips his 360 horses and roars away in his sports car.

Among the fellows he visits with on these rare returns to the neighborhood is another young man of roughly the same age. This one never quite got it together. He wakes up in a hallway or inside of a parked car everyday. His work is not as clearly defined; however, his daily goal is. He must come up with $40 to $60 to get the monkey off his back. He promises himself that he is going to get it *clean*—without hurting anyone. He begs, borrows, cons, charms, pleads and, finally, threatens or steals to *get over*. Sometimes employing daredevil acrobatic feats, he climbs through fire escapes, enters homes, stores or offices. As a last resort, he will put a knife at someone's throat to raise the money for his cure. His daily bread consists of nine parts sugar and one part heroin, to which, he believes, he's addicted and which brings ecstasy and untold dimensions of fulfillment. He is scruffy and bag-eyed. Sometimes he remembers *making the scene* with Pupo. No more.

These are some of the people of El Barrio—each one a universe unto himself, each one only glimpsed here, and each one with dimensions beyond the facade herein described. They all are a part of this neighborhood landscape.

El Barrio is where the Puerto Ricans first came to get their taste of America, to fulfill their dreams of prosperity, to ply their trades and test their mettle against fate, to build their empires, to find their futures, to seek and conquer new worlds and to challenge destiny. They came by the boatloads, hauled across a chunk of ocean and deposited on a Brooklyn pier. Here is where they sunk their roots before embarking on other adventures into America.

Tar Beach

Mostly, we lived life in a crowd. Mostly, we lived life in a crowd because we all had large families. Mostly, we lived life in a crowd because our large families lived in small apartments. Mostly, we lived life in a crowd because there were at least three kids (sometimes more) in each family. Mostly, we lived life in a crowd because there were at least four apartments on each floor of the buildings where we lived. Mostly, we lived life in a crowd because all the buildings where we lived had at least four floors. Mostly, we lived life in a crowd because our families also included relatives that came from Puerto Rico and had nowhere else to go until they found a job. Mostly, we lived life in a crowd because there were no jobs in Puerto Rico for our relatives, and they could find one in New York City. Mostly, we lived life in a crowd because *El Barrio* was where we all came to live when we got to New York. Mostly, we lived life in a crowd because when all of us kids got out of our apartments at the same time, we were a crowd.

Mostly but not always.

Sometimes, I found time to be alone. Sometimes, the only place to be alone was on *Tar Beach*. Sometimes, the only place to be alone was on *Tar Beach*, in the summer. Sometimes, the only place to be alone was on Tar Beach, in the summer, when the sun was coming up. Sometimes, the only place to be alone was on Tar Beach, in the summer, when the sun was coming up and the wind was blowing. Sometimes, the only place to be alone was on Tar Beach, in the summer, when the sun was coming up and the wind was blowing, and my kite was ready to fly!

Sometimes!

Tar Beach" was my rooftop. This was one of those sometimes!

"Ready to fly" meant different things to different people. For some, it meant little more than a kite, a string, and a tail. Others added frills like flaps that sounded in the wind; still others painted colors or symbols; others still, extended the tail or created new shapes or arched the bow. That was Bacalao's thing.

Bacalao—he was El Barrio's legendary kite master. He was also a kite bully, flaunting his considerable skills, cutting down everything in his path and controlling the sky in and around the downwind area for several blocks. He flew a *bacalao*, an oversized diamond, with a long, long tail. He called her simply "El Bacalao," smugly suggesting that his kite was male in gender and a warrior by nature—an affront to the aficionado's time-honored custom of naming kites in the female gender for their grace and beauty. He used triple gazettes and flexed his bow with a skewed curve that gave it the ability to dive, curl back and rise to great heights with swift, sweeping movements. He also put flaps on all four of its sides that roared when he dove. Many skilled assailants had challenged and failed to down El Bacalao over the years. Most had lost their kites, *ajusta*, adrift in the wind after the challenge. Others limped home in disarray or simply pulled in when El Bacalao took to the sky.

My own kite was different. I called her my *"Jade Diamond"* or *"La Diamante de Jade"* for her teal-green color. Others called her "The Diamond from Hades." She was small, but I double papered her to give her more weight, so she could support her twin tails. Each of her four sides was exactly even: eight meticulously measured inches of weighted glass cord wound around and tied to two crossed bamboo rods, glued, taped, and stapled together with equal care and equal weight. The double layer of paper was also carefully measured, folded down and glued in place, one layer at a time, with the exactness tempered into me from five seasons of lost kites and two back-to-back successful ones. Both of her tails were armed with several crossed, double-edged razor blades set firmly and sealed in matchsticks. These matchsticks were wound with thin wire, taped in place on the tail to resist the pressure of any opponent's triple-strength string coated in melted cola glue mixed with ground glass. This was what she flew on, and that was the customary battle armor of kites, should they cross contact with another in a tug of war for supremacy in the sky. That's what "ready to fly" meant to me.

And she was ready to fly!

My first disappointment came when I stepped onto the roof. The wind was blowing from the west. With the wind at my back, I would be looking into the sun. I would have to break one of the cardinal rules of kite battle: never fly into the sun. No matter.

It was a beautiful, warm summer day. A few puffs of grey drifted across the sky, offsetting the azure expanse that defined infinity, the horizon ragged edged by the New York skyline. A few early risers were already aloft. Kites were darting to and fro in the morning breeze. A blue *toro* with a long tail and twin orange *diamonds* sailed along about a block away.

Then, abruptly, the roar of the neighborhood nemesis, El Bacalao, could be heard as he took a steep dive from overhead downwind to the southwest, out of my original line of sight. Bacalao held him in his dive to gain the maximum, fearsome effects of his wing flaps resounding in the wind. No doubt the others heard since they were downwind of him and were his most likely prey. He was pulled up then, following the dive with a swift, dramatic climb that turned every head. He was claiming his turf, warning all others to leave or do battle.

The *toro* was pulled up and guided away, far to the left, on a taut line, keeping clear of El Bacalao's path and range. Since its launching rooftop was upwind and it could be pulled back in from the downwind position to keep clear, the *toro* limited its new flight patterns to small curls and upswings in abbreviated flight paths, careful not to drift downwind in front of El Bacalao again.

The two twin *diamonds* were not as fortunate. The farthest diamond simply paid out more string and drifted away into the horizon, challenging El Bacalao to follow since she had at least a full city block distance. Undeterred, El Bacalao met the challenge. He pulled to a greater height and then executed a long, sweeping controlled drift, with occasional tugs to guide his path as he took aim at the distant *diamond* prey.

Meanwhile, the second *diamond*, which had begun to pull up and pull in, giving way to the original threat, suddenly executed a sharp right sweep and a controlled drift. This brought her racing toward El Bacalao's line, which had stretched past her in pursuit of the first *diamond*. Now the second *diamond* had a direct shot at El Bacalao's line. She swept in and curled up, drawing her tail against El Bacalao's line, her razors reflecting sunlight. Instead of pulling in, El Bacalao let out more line, controlling his drift and avoiding a taut line. The *diamond* pulled up, up and up, but El Bacalao's line just rose with her climb, without sufficient tension and pressure to fix against the blades. Now, the *diamond* tried to pull and dive. Her tail curled up against El Bacalao's, line pulling her out of her dive. She tried to reverse direction. This caused her to rise and turn in the opposite direction, crossing her line with El Bacalao's line. El Bacalao pulled up.

El Bacalao's glass cord ripped through the *diamond's* line like putty. Suddenly, the *diamond* dropped. For a moment, its tail snagged on El Bacalao's line and then off it drifted with the wind.

"Ajusta!"Bacalao called out in triumph. He shouted it from his rooftop to the streets below and the sky above, sending children downstairs racing through the street after the fallen warrior. He then pulled up El Bacalao and executed a full 360-degree circle in the sky, dove, drifted and caused it to pirouette in a victory dance. Then he pulled him into a climb, way, way up to the sky.

Watching the orange *diamond* drift away and sink from sight, I felt the sky weigh down on me. All the empty space spread around and above me, reminding me of my insignificance in the great scheme of the universe.

The *diamond* drifted, dropped and disappeared from the sky amid the tenements of El Barrio. Some fortunate kid would probably chase it down and, if it survived the clawing, clutching and fighting to keep it, would have a good trophy. It might even fly again under someone else's banner. For now, it was history—another conquest for El Bacalao, another notch on his belt, another sad boy running home without his kite, and another war story to ring through the hallways and street corners that recorded the exploits and adventures of El Barrio's youth.

Meanwhile, the blue *toro* in the controlled flight had witnessed El Bacalao's success and decided not to chance an encounter. She was pulled in, making a last controlled loop before landing.

El Bacalao showed pure disdain now, as the sky was clear for the next attack on the fading first *diamond* that was now barely an orange dot in the blue vastness above the skyline. The distance did not fool Bacalao, the kite master. He took aim, not at the kite but at the *diamond's* flyer, who stood on a rooftop across the street and six buildings further along the block. That distance didn't measure a full city block. Bacalao didn't need the whole distance to the kite if he could see or calculate where her line was!

And there was more! Seasoned flyers would give their kites lots of slack for distance—tie her down and then prepare a second kite for launch at the other end of the roof, upwind from his first kite. This ambush kite could then counterattack the stalking kite that would now be on an extended line chasing the first kite. Then there were the *slingshots, bolos* and *skyhooks* to ensnare or cut down pursuing kites whose lines came near a flyer's roof. Once the battle was on, it was on! El Bacalao needed to avoid these defenses.

Bacalao had his own unique defenses as well. He shared the roof with Gallego, the loan shark and numbers runner whose hobby was breeding and flying pigeons. His coops housed over one hundred *homers, tipletts, tumblers, baldies,* and myriad pure-bred pigeons that he collected and trained for work and play.

Bacalao now walked across his roof with his line, giving him a new angle where he was far to the left and still upwind of the *diamond*. He pulled further up to gain even more elevation before he started to drift down toward the *diamond* twin kite, avoiding the flyer's roof with his line while calculating the angle of the *diamond's* line.

He now started his drift, controlling its direction but giving his Bacalao maximum speed and range. When he had dropped low in his drift and was almost level with a distant rooftop along the line of sight of the *diamond*, he pulled up sharply, leaning El Bacalao at a forty-five-degree angle as he climbed and brought his long tail trailing him across the sky. It was over before anyone could tell. In an instant, his tail razors cut smoothly through the *diamond's* line without a hitch.

"Ajusta!" Bacalao again called out his victory chant. El Bacalao then lifted and climbed. He did his 360-degree full circle, dive, drift and pirouette. Then he rose, curled in again and drifted backward in his second victory dance.

The first *diamond* just kept drifting in the distance, probably landing in the East River. Now, Bacalao, the kite master began to pull his kite in closer—aloft, alone and arrogant in his dominion of the sky.

I waited and watched. I was undecided. I considered a quick, measured launch from my upwind position before El Bacalao became aware that I was behind him. I could dive in and pull up with my double tails and multiple blades. Surely, I could cut him down and escape with my speedy *Jade Diamond*. The sun rose slowly. I could hear the gurgling and cooing of Gallego's pigeons on Bacalao's rooftop. They were anxious to be released, but Bacalao wouldn't let them go until Gallego arrived. This would be the time to strike. Then I got my second disappointment. Gallego appeared in the rooftop doorway. He began feeding the birds, and more importantly, he spotted me. I watched Bacalao as he turned slowly to meet my gaze. He smiled, and then he looked up at El Bacalao while he tugged at his line, first to his left and then down and around to the right, executing a perfect figure eight. The smile never left his lips as he turned away.

He had seen me and invited me to the dance.

In the distance, a solitary television antenna stood sentry on a rooftop, guarding a special entrance to the future—a portent of things to come and a warning that tomorrow's television culture would change the rooftop landscape and drive kite flying into oblivion by the sheer numbers of antennae alone and the automobile culture would force the childhood games like stickball and stoopball off the streets of El Barrio.

But my thirteen-year-old mind harbored no such concept as I hesitated, measuring my odds against the veteran kite master, Bacalao, and his adult supporter, Gallego. Whatever advantages I might have enjoyed as I developed my early morning strategies were gone. The sharp-eyed Gallego had stripped the element of surprise from me. The sun would be in my eyes. I had no upwind allies, and he had no downwind targets to occupy his attention.

Was I willing to risk my painstakingly crafted *Jade Diamond* against the legendary kite master and his fearsome El Bacalao? Dared I go mano a mano against the man and the kite that had dominated the sky for a decade?

As if on cue, the answer came in a heartbeat. El Bacalao zoomed down, flaps roaring his challenge in a sharp dive. He had brought his line from above his head across his chest and down to his ankles, held it there and then released his line so that he danced backward in the wind until he pulled him aloft again and around in a quick climb, curling now to the right, executing a full 360-degree circle and another taunting drift dance. He owned the sky. Like hell he did.

My *Jade Diamond* leaped into the air when the next surge blew in from the west behind my back. I released her as soon as I felt the string pull taut and watched her rise while the string slipped through my fingers, its glass coating tearing at the band aids I had wrapped around my fingers and palms for protection.

Bengie, my silent, mixed-mutt companion, had followed me up to the roof. He stood on his hind legs, peering over the edge, his eyes riveted on the flock of pigeons. They were lifting off at the urging of their trainer, Gallego, who had opened their cages and swept the coops with his long bamboo pole to send them swarming in my path like fighter planes entering a sortie in support of El Bacalao.

Now El Bacalao gave way, drifting from her heights with the wind. Inviting me to chase her as the first *diamond* had done. The pigeons swarmed around in a large circle pattern, guided and urged on by Gallego's sharp whistles and sweeping bamboo rod. The flock in flight avoided El Bacalao and the roar of his flaps. But they were not deterred by the silent *Jade Diamond*, creating a formidable moving barrier to her pursuit. She dove and drifted and then swept to her right trying to line up El Bacalao's line. As she did so, Gallego stepped out from behind a pigeon coop. In his hands, he held a fly rod, a fishing pole used by fishermen and meant for casting weighted bait that flies long distances across streams, rivers and lakes to catch trout, bass and other game fish. He leaned back and, with a single motion, swung the rod, releasing the weighted hook in a high, wide arc toward the *Jade Diamond's* line. I reacted as quickly as possible, bringing her down below the roof over the building's edge, in the narrow space between buildings, and then quickly up again in a steep fast climb, avoiding the fly rod's fish line. The fish line arced over to another rooftop and tangled onto a clothesline.

As she climbed, the *Jade Diamond* zipped into the circling, swarming flock of pigeons. Crash! The pigeon barely hesitated in flight, and the *diamond* continued her climb, but the collision caused a rip in her paper. The double layer held, but the rip in the front layer caused a pocket of air to form between the layers! She began to slow in her ascent, and I knew that Bacalao would take immediate advantage in some way.

Time was now on his side. I needed to act quickly before the breach expanded and limited my only advantages of speed and mobility. Now, the *Jade Diamond* had reached a zenith; above and to the right of El Bacalao, I tugged her into a sharp dive further right, giving slack so that she would drift after the dive and cross over El Bacalao's line. El Bacalao responded by pulling into his own climb, but the kite master ran quickly across his rooftop so that our lines no longer crossed. Instead, he brought it under and then above my *diamond* while I was drifting. He suddenly pulled El Bacalao into a steep climb and drew his tail across my line. Now it was my turn to drift further down, paying out my line, to reduce the pressure for his blades. He was relentless. He continued the climb, pulling as taut as he could, shortening his line until he was almost straight up overhead. Gallego was on the other side of the roof, still struggling to get his fly rod free from the clothesline across the way.

My *Jade Diamond's* line was draped over El Bacalao's tail blades like the two sections of a suspension bridge. It was my turn now to climb. El Bacalao had reached his highest point. Any further and he would be pulled into the wind and go into a spin. I jerked my line and my *Jade Diamond* responded. Up she came swiftly and surely, my line sliding along El Bacalao's blades but not giving him any cross-grip or tension that he could cut into. El Bacalao now tried another maneuver. Going into a slow drift, he released and then pulled up violently, looking for the tension between his blades and my line. But my *Jade Diamond* was on the climb, and the violence of his counter move pulled El Bacalao over his zenith. His curved bow slipped under the wind and tumbled forward, roaring out of control. Our lines crossed, El Bacalao trying to pull out of a spin and my *Jade Diamond* trying to gain the height to bring him down. The two lines tugged against one another. Now it was a test of glass cord.

Time stood still.

Suddenly, Gallego came running across his rooftop. He had freed the fishing line from the clothesline! Frantically, he wound his reel up, positioning himself to cast his fishing line at the *Jade Diamond*. But my *Jade Diamond* ripped forward, continuing her climb. She was clear of the tangle.

El Bacalao tumbled. He roared and crashed through the circling flock of pigeons, spinning and whirling, continuing his descent to the street below. The kite master tried to grab his tail to haul it back as it crossed the rooftop. But he only succeeded in crashing into Gallego, knocking him over and preventing him from casting at my *Jade Diamond* and cutting his own fingers on El Bacalao's tail razors. He let go and lifted his bleeding hands, screaming in agony as El Bacalao dropped to the street, chased by the kids below.

"Ajusta!" The cry went up from the surrounding rooftops and the street below!

I let my line out until there was no line left, and then I pulled her in slowly, simply. No other kites rose within her sphere. Majestically, she climbed to her pinnacle and then started her slow descent as I wound her cord onto my bamboo rod in the figure eight pattern, as was customary. She made no victory dance, no sweeps or curls or dives or dances, no loud roars or whistles, and no angry shouts or chants. That vast, blue expanse of sky was hers alone. My *Diamante de Jade* prevailed. She ruled the sky.

I looked back as I departed the roof. The pigeons were back in their coop. Bacalao and Gallego were gone. The blue *toro* was rising to my left, and several other kites were also going up from other rooftops.

Mostly, we lived life in a crowd. But sometimes . . . sometimes I found time to be alone.

This was one of those times.

El Sueño

QUE MILAGRO! QUE PLACÉR!
ENCONTRARLA, SIN SABÉR . . .
Y EN EL ALMA REVIVÍR . . .
UN INFINITO SENTÍR . . .
QUE TAPÓ CON LA DISTÁNCIA
Y EL TIEMPO QUE PASÓ . . .
SIEMPRE, SIEMPRE AÑORANDO
ESE SUEÑO QUE SE ESCAPÓ . . .

CON CORAZÓN MUY LLENO . . .
IMAGINACIÓN SIN FRENO . . .
DE LA GLORIA SOÑANDO . . .
PASÓ EL DIA CANTANDO . . .
COMBINÓ LO SPIRITUÁL
CON LO ACTUÁL . . . Y LO CUADRÓ . . .
SIEMPRE, SIEMPRE AÑORANDO
ESE SUEÑO QUE SE ESCAPÓ . . .

EVITANDO LOS ENCUENTROS . . .
ESCAPANDO LOS EVENTOS . . .
POR NEGÁR LA REALIDÁD . . .
APOYANDO LEALTÁD . . .
POR NO OFENDÉR SU GENTE . . .
DE SU BARRIO SE UYÓ . . .
SIEMPRE, SIEMPRE AÑORANDO
ESE SUEÑO QUE SE ESCAPÓ . . .

AL REGRESO, SOLITARIO . . .
COMO UN SÉR ORDINARIO . . .
VIEJOS PASOS CAMINANDO . . .
NUEVAS VISTAS ENCONTRANDO . . .
FUE IMPOSIBLE OLVIDÁR
ESE TIEMPO QUE AMÓ . . .
SIEMPRE, SIEMPRE AÑORANDO
ESE SUEÑO QUE SE ESCAPÓ . . .

LO QUE TRAIGA EL FUTURO . . .
SEA FUERTE, SEA DURO . . .
VIVIRÁ CON MUCHO GUSTO . . .
TRATARÁ SER SIEMPRE JUSTO . . .
HAMÁS ABANDONÁR PRINCÍPIOS . . .
QUE EN LA VIDA LE SIRVIÓ . . .
SIEMPRE, SIEMPRE AÑORANDO
ESE SUEÑO QUE SE ESCAPÓ.

The Artist

The "artist"—think about it. Conjures up all kinds of images, doesn't it?—stereotypical images of bearded eccentrics, supersophisticates, graceful effeminates, high-strung beauties and long-haired, sandal—and faded jean-wearing cavorters. The images crash against one another on the strength of their variety, disparity and individuality. How does one attempt to confine so many definitions into one conceptualization—one word—"artist?

What is the commonality that links Rafael Tufino, a freelance bohemian whose work hangs in the Metropolitan Museum of Art and who is as at home in the woods of Massachusetts as in the streets of El Barrio and the Puerto Rican countryside, with, say, Graciela Rivera, an operatic performer supreme whose musical vibrancy has graced audiences around the world? What bond exists, for example, between a Pedro Pietri of *Puerto Rican Obituary* fame and Aspirina, the lusty, colorful "Hemingway of El Barrio," who went to his early grave having bequeathed fifty unpublished manuscripts to his wife and eight children, none of whom could read beyond grammar school level? And of what significance is this question to the average Puerto Rican whose knowledge of or interest in the arts can be a passing fancy or a burning passion? And why should anyone take time out to write about it? Or read about it?

The artist has a special talent. It matters not whether it is intrinsic in the person's innate psyche or whether it has been learned at university or through the process of apprenticeship and repetition. However acquired, by its very nature and definition, it must be expressed. It is that precisely—that need to express—that defines the artist, and provides the common psychical phenomena that all artists share. Whether it be the grotesquely molded figures that leap out at you from Jorge Soto's notebook, the intimate whisperings of Julia De Burgos's poetry; or the sensuous, heady images and rhythms from the pen of Rafael Hernandez, the common denominator is the indomitable spirit of expression.

Since the artist, in practicing her art, regardless of which form, exercises absolute freedom of choice in subject matter and treatment. This freedom, in its will, is godlike and unrestricted. Yet, in its form, it must be tempered by some discipline—philosophical, political, moral, religious, cultural and historical or otherwise based on a human experience. The artist is responsible to everyone, but only as his choice within the discipline. That is the significance of the artist's expression to the casual observer as well as to the aficionado—to please, to challenge, to horrify, to invoke the myriad of emotions, to translate beauty, to interpret life and to share a vision.

The special ability a Puerto Rican artist brings to the world carries a responsibility of choices, transmitting to the observer not only a wealth of rich cultural heritage that is our past, but also the reality of our present and the expression of creativity and unconquerable energy that will define our future.

La Pompa

At first, I thought it was the Italian guys. But now that I have thought about it some more, I think it was the Irish. I'm pretty sure it wasn't the Jewish guys because they always give out biblical names like Abraham and Isaac. Italian guys didn't name too many important people Johnny either. Nah, it had to be the Irish who first called me Johnny. I'm really not sure, you know, but it was probably them. I mean, who else would name a pump anything? You know what I mean?

I know, I know, I'm at the bottom of the life chain. I'm an inanimate object that just stands there day after day, after week, after month, after year, after century, so on and so forth. Telephone poles are at least made out of wood. They are only once removed from their natural state in the life chain as trees. Even signs and sign posts are closer to the life chain than I am. They just stand there, like I do. But at least they serve a function every day. You know what I mean. People read them and stuff. Even gates made out of the same stuff I'm made of—cast iron—starting out as trees, compressed into the ground for centuries and scooped out and burned at molten heat just like me. Molded and hammered into all kinds of shapes and designs. Some of them even get to become works of art. But they get to do their work everyday—keep people in and keep people out. See what I mean?

About the life chain? I mean, hey, some of my cousins have been in the same spot for what seems like forever. They never get to do anything—no fires, no street cleaning and not even a dog to pee on them. I mean, I'm not saying that being peed on by a dog is any great shakes. Don't get me wrong now. But at least that was a function in some creature's life. Get my drift?

So getting back to my story, it's about my friend Angelo. He's been my best friend. I mean, I got lots of friends, you know, but mostly these guys are firemen. You know, they are work relationships, not really friends; you know what I mean? Wham! Bam! They come. They hook up the hoses. They put out the fire. And zap, they're gone. No hello. No good-bye. No name. No nothin'. I mean, I like my job, and I do it well. I save people's lives and all. But you know a little pat on the back now and then would be nice.

Don't misunderstand me now. I'm not trying to be a wise guy or nothing, see? I'm really very proud about it. I mean, have you ever heard of a lamppost with a name? Or a stoop? Or a sign post? I mean, sure, some people put plaques and things on benches, right? But, hey, those plaques have the names of the people who dedicated them.

You know, like "In memory of Fulano de tal" and things like that. You know? But to have a name like "Johnny Pump," that's an honor. That's my name, not "In honor of Johnny Pump." Nothing like that. Just plain old "Johnny Pump." Whoa, I mean, they gave me that name. It's mine. It's me.

Angelo was the first guy I heard call me that. But he said it like he had heard it before. You know what I mean? Not like "I name you Johnny" or anything like that. See Angelo was Puerto Rican. So it couldn't have been him 'cause the Puerto Ricans weren't into naming things in English then. I mean in the 1940s. Besides, Angelo was a kid. The way he said it was like it was a known fact. He said, "Don't you guys know what a 'Johnny Pump' is?" Like that! Bam, a known fact!

Besides, the Puerto Ricans called me something else. They call me "La Pompa." Can you believe that? They took my "Johnny" away from me. La Pompa. Wow! What's up with La Pompa? Why not "El Pompo?" That at least is masculine. I mean, my name is Johnny, you know. Get it? Johnny? Masculine? But you know what? I used to be mad at first. I mean, can you blame me? Whoa, hey, La Pompa? What's that all about? But I found out; it's a term of affection. Can you dig that? Affection! Man, now that is something! It's even better than a name. I mean, I love my name. But affection? Whoa, feelings, man, feelings. That's what affection is all about. You gotta hand it to them Puerto Ricans; they bring passion to the game.

La Pompa!

Plus, if Angelo knew that, at the time, he wouldn't have called me Johnny Pump now, would he? I don't mean to be tooting my own horn here now. But I just wanted to set the record straight. So, now you know I have a name, and I am regarded by some with affection. So let's get off that subject, okay? Tell you what, here's the deal. See, I'm here all the time. All kinds of things happen around here. I just wanted you to know that. I mean, I was the first to see Ebaríto fall in that legendary fight way back in the 1940s. You know the story Jack Agüeros wrote about? Over the Domino game, out front here, remember? See, Jack's my friend too, not just Angelo.

And I was right there when Sonny Corleone took out that guy that beat up his sister in *The Godfather*. Remember? In fact, I'm in the movie, just a cameo, of course. But hey, I mean, whaddayou expect? I'm not Al Pacino, you know. I never got paid or anything, but if you look closely, you'll see me. Anyway, it turns out the guy marries Sonny's sister. In the movie, I mean. Even after that whipping! Man, people are weird. Not just in the movies either.

I've seen some good things too. But wait a minute, I was telling you the story about Angelo. Here's the deal. Angelo was just a kid when it all happened. He was new around the block. His family moved here from the Italian section. Actually, the whole neighborhood used to be an Italian neighborhood.

There were still some Italian guys around too. I mean, Danny, Dominic and Louis—they were some of the guys from the block, you know what I mean? Heck, they were on our first softball team and great players too. But that's when the Puerto Ricans started to move in. Man you know, when them Puerto Ricans move in, they move in in droves. Whoa, you look up one day and bam! They are here. Swoop, they took over the neighborhood. Zap! Just like that. There's so many of them. They come in families, in clans, in crowds and in swarms. Boom! They are here, and they let you know it. They make noise; man, do they make noise. But you know what? They don't all make noise; it's just that the ones that do make enough for the hundreds of others that don't. And, after all, you can't hear the quiet ones when the noisy ones are doing their thing, can you? That's just an observation, you know. It ain't got nothing to do with the story. Back to Angelo.

He was a good-looking kid—handsome actually, even in his early teens. He was husky and athletic and fun loving. He was loud and boisterous too. He was one of the loud ones—always attracting attention, mostly from the girls. They couldn't resist him, and he knew it. So he played at it to the max. But he had some problems adapting to the guys on the block, mostly because the guys had some lifestyle things that Angelo didn't fit into yet like *stoopball*, which was a daily pastime. It was a cultural tradition in El Barrio. An adaptation of baseball played without a bat. Instead, a pink rubber *Spalding* ball was used. It was banged fiercely against the concrete molding at the base of a building's wall at a spot designated as *home plate*. The ball would then bounce off the molding, either on the ground or in the air, toward the opposite sidewalk. From that *home plate*, the diamond ran across the street with the *second base* directly on the other sidewalk and the *first* and *third bases* in the middle of the street at forty-five-degree angles from the home plate and *second base*. Some guys played off of the actual stoop—that's why it was called *stoopball*—but not on our block. I mean, if you hit off the stoop, where would they sit down? See what I mean? There had to be a place to sit, so people could watch the game, you know. Yeah, yeah, I know. How come they didn't call it wall ball? Don't be a wise guy, okay? It's the same game. Some guys called it "off the wall." Does that please you? Forget it, man. It's *stoopball*. I don't care where they hit the ball or where they put *home plate*, okay?

Angelo played, but he couldn't quite get the sidearm throw against the wall quite right. He threw the ball down overhand and couldn't catch the point of the molding well enough to produce the desired line drive that most often turned into a base hit. Instead, he hit a *slug* and was *out* most of the time. A slug was an automatic out. And he didn't ever take time to learn the rules and the protocols. I mean, you know, I was more important in the *stoopball* games than he was, and I wasn't even playing! I was just a foul line and a spectator in all these goings-on. But I mean, you know, I had a role in the proceedings. If the ball hit me or passed on my left it was a fair ball. If it passed on my right, it was a foul. I mean, what's a stoopball game without foul lines? Right? But this guy, he just played with this flair and abandon that didn't conform to the standards and ground rules the rest of the guys had established; sometimes he would chase a guy down on the base paths instead of throwing to the player assigned to the base, which usually resulted in a botched play that should have been an *out*. Or he might throw to the wrong base or at the runner, or he would step on the base when he was supposed to tag the runner or vice versa. Sometimes, when he hit the ball, he would keep on running from base to base with no idea if he were *out* or not, often passing a runner in front of him and causing an out—the guy was kind of *nuts*, you know. I mean, whoa, for a new guy on the block, that was not the best way to start new friendships.

But somehow, I felt like he was somebody special, and I mean, he was always hanging around me and hopping over me, so I felt a kind of kinship with him. In his happy-go-lucky way, he just kept on playing and never realized he had caused his team to lose the game. So when the guys chose up sides, they seldom picked him.

He needed something dramatic to build his reputation and develop the comradery that existed among the guys. And you know what? Because he was such a friendly, outgoing, crazy guy, he did it without realizing it. What can be better than that? Here's the deal. This guy has a bunch of brothers and sisters. And the sisters are all tens, got that? *Tens*! Now I gotta tell you, in case you haven't figured it out yet. Guys with them kind of sisters don't need to know how to play *stoopball*. Get my drift? Whoa! They don't need to play nothin'! If you got sisters that are tens, you got more friends than you need! Man, you got friends no matter how many outs you make! You got friends even if you never hit a line drive in your lifetime! Have I made my point?

But, there's more to Angclo than that. He's got character. This is a guy who has got to make his own way. He's not going to let his sister's good looks carry him through life. You know what I mean? Plus, he has skills that had yet to be seen by the guys. And as you probably guessed, I wouldn't be telling you this story if I didn't know it firsthand. And of course, if not for me, it wouldn't be a story at all.

You see, Angelo's family had moved into the block during the past winter. Lots of folks were moving in and out of the block in those days. There were still lots of apartments around. Some landlords gave people a couple of months' rent free just to get the tenants to fill vacancies. The tenants would move in and then move out after three months to get the same deal elsewhere. They would do this several times a year to save money. That was before and during the war.

Anyway, I'm getting away from myself. The point is, during the winter, you don't get to know new kids on the block as easy as the summer 'cause now everybody is outside all the time, get it? Now, it was a hot, sticky, muggy New York summer day in 1944, I think it was. Man, was it hot! August! The guys had just finished a game of stoopball and were sitting on the stoop trying to decide whether to play another game.

They were all sweaty and frazzled when suddenly, Angelo leaped out on his fire escape, two flights up. He swung over the railings and let himself down to the first floor, hanging down from the edge and swinging himself over the first floor railing and dropping onto the first floor landing. The dude is whooping and howling like Tarzan: "Aaa . . . ooo . . . aaaa. Aaa . . . ooo . . . aaa."

He repeated the process on the first floor and then swung over to the bottom rung of the fire escape ladder, swung around a few times and dropped to the ground from the first floor. Bam! Right in front of me, the guy dropped. Then he started thumping his chest! I guess some people just don't like staircases. I mean, whoa, this guy meant to impress.

"Aaa . . . ooo . . . aaa . . . hey, guess what I got guys," he announced, full blast. He had gotten everyone's attention.

"Ta ra!" He turned around. Taped to the back of his belt, around his waist, and hidden under an oversized T-shirt was a full-sized monkey wrench. He ripped off the shirt, revealing his physique, and then he untaped the wrench with another howl, "Aaaooo . . . aaa." His performance generated silent awe.

"Watch this," he said. "Haven't you guys ever seen a monkey wrench before?"

More silence.

I gotta tell you, these were a bunch of noisy, rowdy, knock-down, drag-out and boisterous guys he was talking to. Whoa!

But today, they just stopped and stared.

"What's the matter wit you guys anyway?" he bellowed. "I mean, it's hot an' muggy an' you been playin' ball all day. I know you gotta be tired 'n sweaty. Let's open the Johnny Pump! Aaa . . . ooo . . . aaa."

More silence.

"Man, don't you guys know what a Johnny Pump is?" he asked.

That was the first time I ever heard my name. There was no mistake. He said it twice. Now I gotta tell you, I wanted to yell and scream and carry on, just like him. I mean, you know, I suddenly had a name. I mean, d'you know how many fires I had put out? How many streets I had cleaned over the years? Nobody had ever called me by my name. Whoa, man, this was deep stuff!

Anyway, while I was silently reveling at my great discovery, Angelo had stepped over to me and clamped the wrench on my left side waterspout and was turning it open. He was on fire with pride. I could feel his energy. Whoa, what a guy!

Silence from the guys.

Finally, after he had opened the left spout, he loosened the wrench and brought it to my head lug. I mean, opening the spout is nothing if you don't turn on the faucet, right? And what do you think happens when they open the faucet? Swoosh, out poured the water. I was in my glory. I was doing my thing! Johnny Pump was pumping! Man, I let them know what a Johnny Pump could do. I poured it on full blast! Water rushed out of me like Niagara Falls.

"Holy smoke!"

"Hey, man, you can't do that!"

"You gotta be crazy!"

The silence had been shattered. But Angelo was on a roll. He wasn't listening. Here was the real deal. He was in his element.

"Watch this," he said. He stooped down behind me, reached around as if to hug me and locked his hands together. Then he brought them up, under the stream of water I was spouting out and forced the water into an airborne stream, reaching clear across the street.

"C'mon guys, get in," he called as the water showered the street and the opposite sidewalk. I could see that the guys had never seen anything like this before. First one, then another jumped into the shower. In a flash, the guys were all jumping around and racing in and out of the shower of water Angelo was directing across the street. Whoa! This was magical stuff for a bunch of kids miles from the nearest beach or any kind of relief from New York City's relentless summer heat.

By now, all the guys were taking turns directing the shower or under it. One guy used a large tin can opened on both ends to control the flow of water to greater heights and distance. Then, Angelo found an even better solution. He grabbed a milk box, hooked one corner to my head lug and pushed the other corner down through the stream and down to the other side. Then, he walked away and raced in under the shower. Now nobody needed to direct it.

The force of the stream held the box down in place, and the stream surged through the box and formed an arc that reached all across the street. Soon children of all ages were racing to the huge, cooling shower. They came in swimsuits, they came fully clothed and they climbed on each other's backs. They even brought their dogs, their bikes and their skates. The stickball game up the block came to an abrupt end, the players heading for the huge, refreshing shower.

"La Pompa," they shouted gleefully over and over. "La Pompa."

Man, were they happy! I never knew I could bring so much joy to so many youngsters.

After a while though, Rufo, the grocery store owner came over with his own wrench and put an end to the fun.

Nobody protested. After all, Rufo was Mikey's father. And Mikey was drenched from head to toe. Besides, Rufo's store fed the whole block, even when they didn't have any money. Rufo had a little brown envelope for each family with their receipts for food purchases they had made on credit until the next check came. So nobody was going to risk that.

Not even for La Pompa.

But you know what? That didn't matter. I mean, whoa, everything comes to an end, right?

What did matter was that I had a name. I had two names. One was a name name, and the other was a name that conveyed happiness, joy and pleasure. Affection! Can you dig that?

What else mattered is that Angelo was a hero. Forget stoopball! When it was this hot, something different was what was happening. Angelo had brought his *A* game. He had earned his *bones*. He was now one of the guys, and everybody else experienced something new. Another element was introduced to the children of El Barrio.

A new tradition was born for some and passed on for others.

La Pompa.

Otto Lived

Otto lived.
And was that not enough?
"What did he do?" you ask,
As if to judge his worth.
And is it not enough to live?
Why measure not the smiles, caresses;
Even just the words, which comfort shared
And laughter got?
And is it not enough to say he loved?
Otto lived.

Otto Died

Otto lived . . . really! He was among my closest and most trusted friends. He shared wisdom and laughter and a wealth of dreams and ambitions with me, some of which I've achieved in my lifetime and all of which he took with him to his grave.

And it was an early grave. It is unmarked, unknown and unvisited. He was in it before his thirty-second birthday. But he was on his way to it by age seventeen. It was a long, painful and arduous journey. He traveled on a horse with no legs. White powdered it was, and it took him there by needlepoint. He became addicted to heroin during his teenage years, and his mind and life were out of his control and wasted on useless and meaningless pursuits on the streets of El Barrio, in the jail cells of Attica and, finally, on a hospital bed in East Harlem.

Many of us have known a person like Otto, and a great deal of time, energy and money are spent daily by both public and private sources to prevent, combat and rehabilitate the addictions of substance abusers, "junkies," if you will or alcoholics!

Billions of dollars change hands everyday to manufacture and make available in the marketplace substances that people take to abuse their bodies.

And the pusher—what a vile, contemptible villain he is! Not so the liquor salesman. Prohibition repeal saw to that. He is a businessman. Legitimate! Is there a difference?

And what about nonsubstance abuse? What about providers of nonsubstance that has similar, if not graver, effects on people, on their minds or, if not, on their bodies?

What about people who saturate other people's minds with junk? And turn them into intellectual junkies? What difference is there between providing alcohol or other drugs that debilitate and deteriorate a person's body and providing *stuff* that addicts one's mind and nullifies the creativity and purposeful activity of a living being?

Television—the electronic miracle that has transformed the twentieth century society and has, at the same time, become the greatest vehicle for the providers of nonsubstance abuse—the providers of mind-affecting matter that can shape opinion and influence behavior and that can educate or desecrate.

There are many providers whose specific target is the Latino population of the US. They are licensed by the Federal Communications Commission to use the public airwaves to broadcast. And they use that license to transmit to a population rapidly approaching thirty million people. In Spanish, what do they transmit? What effect does what they transmit have on consumers? What opinions does it shape? What behavior does it elicit? What purpose does it serve? Of what value is it?

> A typical week of Spanish language television in New York City, for example, provides 12.5 hours of news;

> 3 hours of public affairs programming; 8 hours of sports; 2 hours of culturally oriented programming (primarily devoted to popular music forms, which vary a little, if at all, from the variety shows described as entertainment programming); and 105 hours of "entertainment programming," which are devoted to a mélange of situation comedies, variety shows, cartoons, old movies and (sigh) soap operas, interspersed continuously and callously with an inordinate number of poorly produced commercials.

Over 90 percent of these programs are imported and prerecorded. Most of them are disgracefully bad productions as well as irrelevant, obnoxious, and totally devoid of purpose, meaning and consequence to the Latino consumer in the US.

Junk! Pure intellectual nonsubstance! The stuff *ODs* are made of.

If Otto had been addicted to this stuff, his body might not be decomposing in a grave, but he would still be nodding in his living room, his life would still be meaningless and purposeless, and he would be a nonsubstance abuser.

How many novela addicts do you know? How many nullified, creative minds and purposeless hours are wasted? If a drug pusher walked into your living room and sat there from 3:30 PM to midnight every weekday and all day on Saturday and Sunday dealing heroin, what would you do? Need I say more?

The irony of it is that it is totally and completely unnecessary by any standards. Bad television has never made as much money as good television, in any language. It never has, and it never will.

Lord & Taylor never was in competition with John's bargain store. On the other hand, why was Gimbel's across the street from Macy's?

The providers of Spanish language television will always have a market, and they can shape opinion in that market and elicit behavior in that market. They can assume responsibility for sharing in the education and the economic and social development of that market, which in turn, will result in greater affluence and, consequently, more and better clientele for the provider, or they can continue the penny-ante, junk peddler approach to television.

There is a wealth of Latino talent in this nation that can contribute to the growth of qualitative and responsible programming in Spanish language television. I see them every day, and I watch them shudder in disgust when the subject of Spanish language television is raised. They can offer an alternative to the mind pollution that rides the public airwaves today. They are perfecting their art and their craft with discipline, precision and plain old hard work because they know one thing for sure—Otto lived!

Across Third Avenue: Freedom

Third Avenue. As far as the eye could see, the cobblestone street was saddled by a great, black, spiderlike iron monster called the "Third Avenue El." It cast a checkerboard shadow, alternating with shafts of sunlight like a huge web draped across the wide boulevard, waiting for unsuspecting victims. I remember sitting on the curb, staring across to the east side of the street, the ominous, foreboding presence of the *El* weighing on my eight-year-old mind and giving more substance to the taboo that Third Avenue was for the Puerto Rican kid in East Harlem.

Across that no-man's land was an unknown world filled with exotic delights and adventures not accessible to me except through hearsay. Somewhere beyond was Jefferson Park and an Olympic-sized swimming pool and the Italian festival of Our Lady of Mt. Carmel, complete with Ferris wheel, merry-go-round, pizza pies, cotton candy, multi-flavored ices, and fireworks; there were a live market, fishing piers that extended into the East River and the Boys Club. That I knew of for certain. The things I didn't know about were endless. My imagination soared as I sat watching the red and gold trolleys rattle along on the shiny silver tracks embedded in the cobblestones and listened to the roar and clatter of the iron horse overhead, spattering sparks into the air.

The traffic wasn't so heavy, and the traffic light was no different from any other. Red meant "stop," and green meant "go." And there wasn't any barbed wire or solid wall or alligator-filled moat or any other physical obstacle to keep me sitting on the curb day-dreaming while other people came and went, oblivious to my vicarious meanderings—none of that. The fact is, with my sneakers, I could probably beat nearly anyone across and back.

No, the barrier wasn't one my wiry body couldn't run under, over or through. The barrier was inside my head—not that it wasn't real. It was real. But it had gotten inside my head the same way the knowledge of Jefferson Pool and the Boys Club had gotten there through hearsay: stories, rumors and countless tales that fill the ether, the *stuff* of which tradition is made, transmitted from one person to another over time and distance. It was accepted fact without ever having been experienced. It was self-fulfilling.

Puerto Ricans were not to cross third avenue; that was Italian territory. Period.

Even Danny—"Italian Junior" we called him then—to this day among my closest and most trusted friends, more a brother than a friend, could not offer a solution.

Beyond third avenue, you risked your life. It was a challenge I grew up with. Over the years the third avenue *barrier* appears to have crumbled under the steady flow of Puerto Ricans into El Barrio and Italians out of East Harlem, not without a good measure of violence and heartache and bloodshed. Yet although the Third Avenue El and the trolleys no longer run on third avenue and although the movement of Puerto Ricans in and around New York seems, on the surface, to have overcome the *barrier*, remnants of it still linger. The wall of *unwelcome* still survives, for some. As always, it is invisible. It came to us through tradition and through institutional behavior—it is the lifestyle of America. It can be traced back through the various ebbs and flows of waves and waves of immigrants who were nursed on an institutional inferiority syndrome that required them to cast away their cultural values to assume the American identity.

I am not suggesting that this behavior was peculiar to Italians in East Harlem. No such luck. Had it been that way, it would have been easy to deal with. No, they learned it here as a result of their experience as newcomers. And others had learned it before them, and they, in turn, learned from their predecessors. That's what tradition is. That's how social institutions are built.

In those days, I never questioned the pennies dropped into the church basket or the coins for the poor box that mom gave us ritually on Sunday, although our table seldom saw a chicken or a pork chop. That too was tradition.

In the midst of the roar of bricks launched from a rooftop and zip gun blasts in the night, we were learning in school that George Washington never told a lie, Abraham Lincoln freed slaves and every child in America could grow to be president. We learned it all by rote ("Four score and seven years ago our forefathers brought forth upon this continent a new nation conceived in liberty and dedicated to the proposition that all men are created equal."). Those words reverberated through my mind on many occasions: while I heaved a garbage can down hard and heavy on some bastard who I'd knocked to the ground before he got to me and when I rolled in the gutter, tasting blood and dirt while someone's booted foot dug deep into my ribs and spine.

But I never grew up bitter.

I grew up hauling blocks of ice up five flights for the little old Italian lady who lived next door, running every conceivable kind of errand for anybody who needed it and translating for Mrs. Rivera and Mr. Gonzalez to the teacher, the insurance agent, the welfare investigator, the cop, the landlord, the nurse, the truant officer, etc. "What a good boy you have, Maria," all the neighbors said. And I was.

And I grew up getting my ass kicked and kicking the next guy's ass up and down the streets of El Barrio. "That's a bad dude, Chino," the reputation went. And I was.

I grew up knowing that cruelty and violence and deceit were all part of the personal repertoire of social tools that I needed to be armed with to fend off the merchants of hypocrisy that rule and govern and perpetuate the *traditions* that make America *great*. In the vernacular of contemporary American thought, it all comes under the category of *being realistic*.

The idea was never to unleash your weapons until the showdown came. The *good guy*, after all, never drew his gun first in the movies. But when he did, look out.

A strange ethic when you look at it. To be the *good guy*, you had to be able to do all the things that characterized the *bad guy* better than they did. Simplistic? Probably so—it's also what the Watergate mess appears to be about: a self-righteous hypocrisy that led some people to think that they, being the good guys, could use any means necessary to insure that they could continue to be the good guys. Bullshit.

But it's the American way, and it's the system that has been perpetuated in institution after institution, from the church to the Mafia, from the government to revolutionary movements, from the suburbs to the central city and from corporations to united funds.

I'm not going to judge it. After all, even the Watergate came to light, and there may be a remedy for that mess; someone may say, "It was that same system that weeded out the imperfections and developed a solution," and certainly, the traditions and institutions in America seek to resolve the problems they confront. I won't disagree with that.

But history has taught me that the institution that is a solution to one problem quickly becomes, itself, the next problem for which a solution must be found. So it is with churches, armies, the police, museums, corporations, labor unions, newspapers and commissions.

Third Avenue has been with me all my life, and I suspect it will be with all Puerto Ricans all of their lives in one form or another. And it affected and will continue to affect every experience of any significance in my lifetime.

It was there in the military when, after four years as an instructor and guided missiles expert, I was discharged A/2C. It was there in college, which required seven years and three dropouts to complete. It was there in Mississippi when we started *freedom schools* to achieve *equal* education.

It was still there in El Barrio during the rent strike days and community action days when the antipoverty program raised hopes and generated dreams of self-help, only to be ground into the dust of yesterday's rhetoric. And it lived on with the experimental school districts and the struggles for *community control* and the vain attempts to wrest control in a neighborhood shared politically by legislators from other communities but served by none. It was there when the publishers sent rejection slip after rejection slip, and I finally had to raise the bucks to publish my book myself.

It's still there now, when every instrument of mass communications—print and electronic—chooses to ignore the Puerto Rican editorially or carefully selects the images it presents, thus helping to perpetuate stereotypical negativism or promote a token Puerto Rican personality while systematically denying employment and opportunities to Puerto Ricans exclusive of the mail room. In New York City today, you can count on the fingers of your hands the number of Puerto Ricans employed in a professional capacity in all the major television, radio and print media combined.

I suppose I'll always sit on the curb somewhere, staring in the Third Avenues of the world, wanting to belong. And I suppose too that I'll venture forth into that unknown, seeking and probing and discovering. And I expect too that I'll always have my pennies for the poor box, eager to serve and be *good* in what is likely to be a quixotic adventure. But one thing you can count on as absolutely certain: Third Avenue was not and will not be a deterrent to joining the struggle and doing the things that need to be done, or at least trying to do what needs to be done. It can never deter me from choosing to put on my PFs and running under, over or through it.

Borinquen's Barrio Boys

The elegance of morning, golden, pink and blue,
soft and quiet; marking time 'til grown-ups awaken
to mar its beauty with twentieth century confusion
is already stunned out of peacefulness
by frantic children . . . black and brown and pink . . .
fathomless souls; alive and eager to wear out
the bearded man with the scythe.
"Follow the leader," shrieks the piercing goblin voice
in an almost white T-shirt with several holes
as he bounces down the creaking wooden steps
not yet awake and voicing their displeasure.
He leaps and ricochets off dingy, yellow-brown walls
with a million cracks and chipped paint
and chalk and crayon sayings, recording decades
of youthful love: "Pete & Linda," "Chino Loves Vicky,"
"I love Hector." Here thousands of embraces
and caresses some tender, others even brutal led to
happy lives or bastard sons or impoverished marriages.
The sneakered feet tramp on amidst
the snores and groans of half-awakened neighbors,
whose minds are filled with thoughts of sordid ways
to end the bouncing and screeching of the youth who
vibrates walls and rattles windows
with his maddening, frenzied, morning-insulting antics,
catapulting through the half-lit hallway air, gobbling
up the last twelve steps.
In a single soar, lungs in dungarees and sneakers
crackle into the city streets, screaming "Follow the leader,"
while through the magic of childhood communication

a dozen such simultaneous appearances are made,
while shoddy tenements smile through dirty windowpanes
and soot-layered walls.
The grocer sighs deep and hurriedly carries in the
dawn-delivered milk . . .
not quick enough to save two bottles, disappearing . . .
into an alleyway, with a pair of brown, ten-year-old
hands firmly welded to them.
Running, jumping, laughing, talking, in a barbaric
ritual, morning reunion dance the children gather;
a blur of motion in spatial timelessness.
Eager, worn-out rubber-soled sneakers
marry the human skin to
cement sidewalks and asphalt streets
in a holy union tied up with broken shoestrings.
The togetherness of child and street erupts
in a chorus of "Follow the leader."
Into the catacombs of slums plunge the atomic boys
through hallways, basements, and empty lots
to their Shangri-la;
the wonderland of walls and windows and fire escapes
and brick buildings and wooden fences and hiding places.
"El ultimo es pato," they challenge. "The last one is a punk,"
electrifying the morning and starting
the invasion of back lots, which each one
knows like his own soul.
Even vagrant clouds dare not eclipse these beings
from the few streaks of sunshine that break through the
wall of buildings.
"I'm leader!"
"I'm second!'
"I'm third!"
On and on they call out their numbers as they fall into place
for a breathtaking day of daring, bravery, and downright lunacy.
"Over the wall!" shouts the leader as the attack begins
in a clutching, clawing ascent.

Fiery eyes scan the walls for "grips,"
as the lithe, agile bodies climb breathtakingly,
only to leap down on the other side and start anew elsewhere
while bleary-eyed adults are shocked out of their wits
by monkeylike children, swinging from fire escapes,
past bedroom windows onto adjoining buildings.
On through the day, the devilment continues,
occasionally interrupted by insatiable appetites
that send the boys scurrying home in sandwich-devouring
soda-chugging rampages and returns them
bursting with even more energy.
From follow-the-leader to tag to kick-the-can to
chase-the-white-horse to ring-o-leerio
to Johnny-and-the-pony"
to stickball to stoopball to
a myriad street culture of games;
bolting, scampering, rampant children burn through
the summer day. Finally, sweat soaked and strength sapped,
they trudge home heavily to rest as old man Sol blinks wearily
beyond the horizon.

So Nice

We're so nice,
So sweet.
Man, are we sweet:
Got style, culture, couth,
Don't get upset when
We're soothed by dishonest
Dribbling from lifelong cons.

We'll sing,
We'll cry and wring our hands;
But stay so sweet and not
Sustain our furor or our wrath.

It can't hurt long.
If so,
We can withstand
'Til in perpetual
Sleep
Heaven finds us.
So we'll be sweet
And never win our fight.

Puerto Rico Libre

Don't be misled
By constant sunshine on our land
Nor soft sea breezes;
Gentle rolling waves
Upon our shores
Warm ocean; quiet surf.

Invisible to you as winter
Is the force frustration bore
And outrage bred
And hope diffused
And pride restored
And love nurtured
And experience forged
And time enlightened
And imperialism antagonized
And revolution sustains.

La Canción Del Asopao

Era un día bien nublao
Andaba solo y desvelao
No había dormido, y estaba cansao
Cuando nombraron el Asopao

Muchacho! No se qué me ha pasao
Brinqué de pies como un alabao
De donde estaba, salí volao

Con pimientos, cebollas y ajos picao,
Ajices dulces, laurél 'to oreganao'
Añadió cilantro, y hizo un recao
Aceitunas, y acéite, pero no quemao
El sofrito ya había empezao
Arróz y Costillas en vez de Bacalao
Que mas le hecharon se me ha olvidao.

Los otros venian embalao
En un carrito embotellao
De rumbos norte venian prensao
Algunos cómodos, otros tirao
Llegaron todos atropellao
Pero, ni modo, venian preparao

Un Aguacate, fué mezclao
Y un vinito bien brindao
Gozamos la tarde alimentao
Bomba y Plena bien bailao.
La madrugada había llegao
Sin darnos cuenta había pasao
Noche bella y disfrutao
Me despedí muy encantao

Pensando en ellos, yo entusiasmao
Cojí mi pluma como un tumbao
Cantando bajito y de lao en lao
Palabra surjiendo entimbalao
Inventé mi poesia con los ojos cerrao
No fué gran cosa, no fué premiao
Pero con mucho gusto y no sentao
Se la dediqué al asopao
Y, ya tu sabes, p'al otro lao.

La Barberia II

There were four men waiting and two getting their haircuts when Robertito entered the barbershop and took a seat. Felipito, the owner, who normally cut Robertito's hair, was in the back room. His barber chair was vacant. Robertito could hear his voice, together with others, singing and seemingly starting a party back there.

Not too bad, thought Robertito, *with two barbers working at once I should be out of here in less than an hour*. Another hour to do his chores and he would just about make it to the playground in time to start the softball game. He would miss warming up, but what the heck, he was always ready. He fingered his glove, which was strapped to his belt between the strap loops of his pants. He always carried it there in order to leave his hands free for other things. *Man, coach'll probably start somebody else at second base if I miss practice and warm-ups*, he thought. He sat in his chair, waiting his turn and daydreaming different scenarios on the field without him there. He pictured different players at second, making plays. None could cover as much ground as fast as he could. None of them could turn the double play, protect the bag, handle the cutoffs, execute the backhand going away or scoop up the short hop and throw while charging in as he could. Nobody knew the proper way to back up the shortstop or first baseman on certain plays; how to position themselves for particular batters; when to expect a bunt; when and how to call for a pickoff play; how to play the relays and make the throws to the right base—none of that stuff. *None of them guys know all those things I know about the game—none of them*, Robertito thought to himself.

He knew all the moves, all the plays and all the strategies. He knew the game. Period! *I need to get out there quick*, he thought. Other people walked into the barbershop after him, but he knew who the four in front of him were. Among the new arrivals was Rubén, the *bolitero*. He was always among the first to arrive. You never knew if he was there to take bets or to get his haircut—usually both. The shop was filling up fast. There were now more than ten people waiting and making bets. All the waiting area seats were filled, and Robertito was only two people away from his turn. Felipito was still in the back room. Laughter, music and conversation could be heard as some folks came and went, not necessarily having their hair cut. The third barber chair was still unattended.

When Robertito's turn came, he started for the vacated chair, but Rubén jumped up and sat down in the chair.

"Listen," he said to Robertito, "please let me take your turn, I really have an emergency. I have to take my wife to the doctor, and I don't think I can get back in time for my haircut. Please let me take your place."

The little boy looked up at the pleading man. He didn't know what to do. He needed to get to the game, yet here was a grown man pleading to get his wife to a doctor.

"But I was here first," he said. "I've been waiting."

"I know, I know. But I can't wait any longer. Can't you see? It's important. I have to get back to my wife quickly to take her to the doctor. Please let me have your turn, please?"

Robertito looked around the room. "I'll be late for my game," he said, looking around the room for support. Felipito wasn't there, and the other barber just stood there staring blankly at the boy.

"Your game?" exclaimed Rubén. "Your game? My wife has to wait to see her doctor because of your game? You think your game is more important than my sick wife?" Rubén looked around pleadingly at all the people in the shop. "What a selfish little boy you are," he continued, berating the boy. "Look at this selfish kid," he now addressed the rest of the people. "His game is more important than my sick wife," he glared at Robertito.

"It's *okay*," said Robertito. "You can go first. I'm sorry," he barely whispered as he returned to his seat.

"Good," said Rubén. "You're a smart kid," he smiled with satisfaction as the barber began cutting his hair. By now, there was a regular parade of people in and out of the barbershop. Some were going to the back room to join the party; others sat or stood around waiting for haircuts.

Felipito didn't pay any attention. The third barber chair remained empty. Robertito returned to his softball daydreams now. He was imagining different game situations. Now there was a bunt down the first base line. As the first baseman charged in to field the ball, Robertito raced to first base, which was now undefended. The first baseman fielded the ball and whipped it to first base, where Robertito made the play. Next, he imagined the batter hitting a shallow pop fly to right-center field. Robertito, racing back, caught the ball, his back to the plate, turned and fired the ball back to the shortstop, covering second base, where the runner had started to run toward third base, not expecting Robertito to catch the ball. Double play!

The second barber now completed another haircut. As the man rose to leave, another man quickly stepped up and sat in the chair. This man had followed when Rubén entered.

"Hey, mister," said Robertito, "it's my turn."

The man glared down at him and said, "Oh no, you don't. I came in with Rubén. It's my turn right after him."

"But I let Rubén go in my place. It's my turn." Robertito looked pleadingly at the barber, who simply turned around. Felipito was nowhere in sight.

"Look, kid," said the man in the chair, "you gave up your turn. Now you go to the back of the line. That's all to it!"
Robertito looked around the room at the lineup of men waiting their turn. They all stared at him sternly.

"That's not fair," he said. "I was here first."

Rubén, sitting in his chair having his haircut, laughed aloud.

Robertito turned to him. "It's not funny. I gave you my turn, so you could take your wife to the doctor." Tears filled his eyes.

"Wise up, kid," said Rubén. "Everybody knows I'm not married."

The barbershop erupted in laughter. Robertito returned to his seat. Now there was a man sitting in it.

"Sorry," said the man, "you gave up this seat. It's mine now."

Robertito was bewildered. He walked away. "I'm next," he called aloud. "I was here first."

He watched as Rubén finished his haircut. Before anyone else could move, he leaped from his chair and ran to the barber chair and sat down. Another man stepped up.

"My turn is next," he said.

"No," said Robertito. "Rubén took my turn. He lied to me to jump the line."

"I'm sorry about that, but my turn is next. If you missed your turn you have to go to the back of the line like everyone else."

"But you saw me, mister. I was here before you came in. You heard what Rubén did. He lied to get ahead of me. No way I'm leaving this chair. It's my turn, and I'm not moving."

Now, the barber came over and said, "I'm sorry, this gentleman has been waiting, and his turn is after Rubén. You have to wait in line like everybody else."

"But you saw me here first, mister. Rubén lied to me. Call Felipito. He'll tell you."

"Oh, I can't do that. Don Felipito is very busy. If you like, you can go back there and have him come here to decide." The barber winked at the man standing in front of Robertito.

Robertito was caught in a dilemma. If he left the chair, the barber would permit the man to sit down and begin cutting his hair. Felipito was probably drunk in the back room by now and wouldn't listen to him. He would lose his turn again, and now all the others in the shop would expect him to try to get to the chair first after each person was through.

"I'm not moving. You cut my hair now," he said.

The barber didn't respond. Instead, he glared sternly at Robertito. He then moved over to Felipito's chair, nodded to the man, who sat down in the third barber chair. The barber ignored Robertito and began cutting the man's hair.

Now Robertito looked and saw that his seat had been taken by another person. He stayed where he was. He realized that he would never get to the ball game. He couldn't concentrate, so his softball daydreams were gone. Suddenly, he felt the urge to go to the bathroom. He didn't dare leave his seat. He looked around the room. There wasn't a single person who showed any interest in his plight. Several people looked at him and snickered. By now, Rubén had come and gone several times, picking up bets. Each time, he would look at Robertito and laugh aloud.

Robertito sat in place all afternoon, trying to control his bladder. Finally, he lost control of it. He simply sat there, letting the warm liquid flow out of him, soaking him and the barber chair. He would not move. People came and went. He lost track of his place. Nobody paid attention to him. He dared not get up. Finally, one of the barbers came over and offered to cut his hair. He refused. The two barbers finally left, and the front barbershop emptied. Robertito sat in the chair listening to the music and boisterous activities in the back room. Finally, after darkness fell, he got up to leave. Suddenly, the back door opened, and several of the revelers came out, Felipito among them.

Robertito broke out crying.

"Que pasa, mijo?" asked Felipito. "What are you doing here so late?"

Robertito recounted the events of the day.

"We probably lost the game, too," said. "The other guys can't play second base right."

Felipito was perplexed. He was also very drunk and couldn't think very clearly.

"No te apures, mijo," he sputtered. "Come back on Monday. I'll give you a free haircut and see how we can make it up to you. Tell your parents I'm sorry."

Robertito trudged home. His pants were soaking wet. He was tired and hungry, but he took all the backyard and basement paths to get home so that he wouldn't be seen by the guys.

The team had lost the game. All day Sunday, somebody would call him out and heap derision on him.

"Man, what's wrong wit' chu? You knew we had a game. At least you could have told us you weren't coming. Maybe we could have got Peewee or somebody to play second."

"You're a *chump*, man. You made us lose the game!"

"You always talk all that crap about how we're supposed to depend on each other. We waited all afternoon for you. You ain't shit, you know that?"

"So what's up with you. Man, you let us all down. Nobody wants to play with you anymore. You're supposed to be the captain 'n know everything about the game. You don't even know how to *find* the game, *chump!*"

"Listen, *turkey*, you blew it! So don't make no excuses. You are one lame *banana*! You know that?"

Then came his best friend, Danny. "You know what's the worse part? We had a sponsor that was gonna get our uniforms an' equipment 'n' stuff. Plus, he bet a bunch of money on the game 'n' lost it to that bolitero guy, Rubén. He lost about $200 dollars on us, maybe even more. That ain't no joke!"

"What are you talkin' about? *Nobody* got that kind of money to bet on *us!*"

"Yeah, well all them grown men been watchin' our games every week an' notice we always win. So they been startin' to bet on the games. 'Specially Rubén. He's been makin' beau coup bucks on us, an' we didn't even know about it! So that old drunk guy wit' the barbershop bet on us. He said he was gonna get us our uniforms if we won this week. Now, we ain't getting' shit! Thanks to you! *Dufus!*"

Robertito was stunned. Could it be? Could Rubén have planned such a thing? *I'm just a kid. I never did anything to him. I don't even know him. He doesn't know me. What the hell is going on? I better tell Felipito.*

He did. He was at the barbershop first thing on Monday.

Felipito said, "Go away now. I don't want Rubén to see you here, nor my barbers. Come tonight after I close. I'll return and wait inside with the lights out."

Two weeks later, Rubén entered the barbershop, as was his custom. Again the two barbers were occupied, and Felipito's chair was vacant. Two men were waiting their turn. Rubén went to the back room, and let people know that he was taking bets on the numbers. He then took a seat out front to await his turn for a haircut. He continued to take bets as he waited. People came and went. Some bet; some went in the back to drink and sing and make music; some waited for their turn at a haircut.

Robertito entered the barbershop. Rubén laughed aloud when he saw Robertito.

"Well, well," he said, "if it isn't my little baseball player friend."

"I'm not your friend. You're a liar and a thief!"

"Hey, don't talk to me like that. I'll smack you silly." Rubén stood up, taking a step toward Robertito. At that moment, Felipito came in from the back room. Robertito jumped up and ran to Felipito's barber chair. He sat at the edge of it as if ready to bolt, if necessary.

"What's going on here?" Felipito stepped between the two. "You can't behave this way in my barbershop! Here, little boy, step away from that chair. It's Rubén's turn. Come, Rubén, sit down and relax."

Robertito carefully stepped down from the chair and moved around behind it, keeping his distance from Rubén. Rubén moved to the chair and sat down.

"You shouldn't let fresh kids like that in here, Felipito. They can drive your customers away with their foul talk."

"Okay, kid," said Felipito, "don't say another word or I'll have to put you out."

Robertito glared at Rubén but held his tongue. Rubén laughed again and leaned back in the chair as Felipito began cutting his hair.

A few minutes later, the telephone rang. Felipito picked it up.

"¿Que, qué?" he asked excitedly. "When? Where is she? Oh my God, don't tell me that. I'll be right there."

He turned to the people in the shop.

"I'm sorry everybody. I have to close the shop now. My wife has been taken to the hospital. She had a heart attack. Come, everybody has to leave. I don't know when I can come back. It's in New Jersey."

He began ushering the people out and went into the back room to tell the folks back there as well. Everyone got up to leave.

"What about my haircut?" asked Rubén.

"Come back next week. I'll give you a free one," answered Felipito. "Now please go. I have to lock everything up."

Rubén started to get up, but he couldn't move. His shirt stuck to the chair. He tried to lift his feet, but his shoes stuck to the foot supports on the chair.

"Hey, what the hell's going on here?" he exclaimed. "I'm stuck."

"What? What are you talking about?" asked Felipito.
"My damned feet are stuck to the chair. So is my shirt."

Everyone turned to look. Robertito laughed aloud.

"Oh, please, don't be silly Rubén. Come on, I have to leave. I can't be fooling around here," cried Felipito.

"I'm not fooling. I'm stuck!"

"How did that happen? What the hell do you have on your shirt?"

"My shirt? What the hell do you have on your chair? Man, this shirt cost fifty dollars!"

"Look here, don't blame my chair. I clean these chairs everyday when I come in."

By now everyone was roaring with laughter.

"Well, take your shirt off, and let's go. Here, I can lend you one of my barber coats."

"Are you crazy?" yelled Rubén. "My shoes cost two hundred bucks. They're stuck on this chair!"

"Mira, Rubén, I don't know anything about your shirt or your shoes. Only thing I know is that I have to get to the hospital to take care of my wife. So get your shit together and get the hell out of here. I gotta lock up!"

Rubén ripped off his shirt and shoes. But when he tried to raise himself off the seat, he still couldn't move.

"Dammit," he screamed, "my pants are stuck too." He looked up with rage as Robertito laughed with glee in front of the crowd. "It was you, you little shit. These slacks cost me a hundred and fifty bucks."

"Come on, Rubén, move it. Get out of those clothes, and put on this coat. I can't wait any longer. Let's go," said Felipito.

By now, the whole neighborhood had run to the barbershop to see what the commotion was about. Rubén slid out of his trousers awkwardly and stepped out of his shoes. He had only his underpants, no shirt and holes in his socks. He wrapped the barber coat around himself, tied it on and stepped outside into the middle of the laughing, hysterical crowd. Suddenly, he remembered. All his bets were in his pants pocket. He turned back to the barbershop. The door was locked. Felipito was gone.

With his back to the crowd, the barber coat faced the neighborhood. Written in bold back letters it read, "I AM A LIAR AND A THIEF. (P.S. FELIPITO ISN'T MARRIED EITHER!)"

Joe Came

Joe came, and why not?
Yet sadness filled my heart.
For he could not see in his fingertips,
the might to set my people free.
To build; to bring tomorrow to our door today.
To break the shackles that entwines our minds;
that say "I can not," when I know I can;
that offers no rewards, when life itself prays to be shared.
To fill another body with desire and hope;
and dreams of new horizons to be seen.
New dawns which bring new days and dreams forgotten
But not forsaken.
For what else is life but dreams?
Tomorrows found; or not yet wished and sought; or sometimes bought.
But not to have had is not to have lived.
And laughter's not enough,
for Joe, nor me.

Puerto Rican Power

Make way, America, make way.
We're here, and we intend to stay.
We've paid our dues in blood and sweat.
We've hauled our weight and placed our bet.
We've plowed your land and picked your fruit.
We've washed your dishes and breathed your soot.
We've brave the sting of snow and sleet,
Long winter nights without no heat.

While your merchants and landlords picked our pockets,
Our brothers and sisters filled your dockets.
We couldn't do more than stand and stare
As your rodents danced on our tables, bare.
Our valiant sons had their guts blown away
At Normandy, Panmunjom, and Hue.
While a tidal wave of tears were shed
By mothers praying; their children dead.

You've taken our land and polluted our Rivers,
Lived off our backs and ruptured our livers.
Our golden beaches you use for your pleasure
For you, Puerto Rico's your personal treasure.
But our sinews grow strong with our faith in hereafter
And the will to survive turns despair into laughter.
Our loins are aflame with the heat that brings life
And our souls reassured with endurance of strife.

We will not succumb to the burdens of living;
Nor beg simple alms from your patrons of giving.
We'll stand, heads aloft, as our guts churn with anger
We'll carve out our worth though our lives we endanger.
Every single fiber we'll penetrate;
in every city and every state.
We'll buy and sell and win and take.
Every rule we'll learn and others we'll make

We will not stop though our graves fill with flowers
For the whole world knows what you stole is ours
The gauntlet you hurled in '98,
We have picked up to fashion your fate.
We'll own and we'll rule our island nation
As Borinquen spawns her next generation.

I've Got Your Number

Prologue

The show opens with a silent film sequence showing Frankie Cristo on his way home from work. He is characterized as a comic of sorts as he turns the clock forward to 5:00 o'clock (A deceptive rouse to fool the foreman) and leaves his place of employment.

Murphy, the cop, is introduced at this time also. Using separate, silent filming, we see Murphy punching in to go to work. He puts on his uniform and is shown leaving the station.

Simultaneous filming shows Frankie on his way home in the subway and Murphy walking the streets on the way to the opening scene.

Scene One

Frankie is seen getting off the subway and emerging on the street. He sees Murphy standing by the subway entrance. Frankie ducks back into the station and pulls out a false rubber bald head and nose, eyeglasses, and a moustache disguise and puts them on. He exits, walking by Murphy.

Frankie

Halo, police.

Murphy nods. Frankie quickly walks by and heads for his block. Dissolve.

Reopen on a city street facing a grocery store front. To the right of the store is the entrance to a tenement house. On the left is an alley. There is a dice game underway in the alley. Between the entrance and the alley, Papo sits in a milk crate, strumming a guitar and singing while intermittently drinking beer from a can that is concealed in a brown paper bag.

Luis, the store owner, stands at the store entrance. Frankie enters from stage right, wearing his disguise. It is early evening on a warm spring day.

Frankie

Hey! You seen Frankie? (Before they can answer, he removes his disguise and breaks into hysterical laughter.)

"Ha ha! I fool you, no? Ha ha! I fool that dumb cop too! Ha ha! Hey, Papo, you know what everybody hates?"

Papo

No, wha'?

Frankie

Ha ha! A dumb cop—everybody hates a dumb cop! Ha ha!

Papo

What happened, Frankie, Murf after you again?

Frankie

I guess so. He was by the subway station. Has he been by here yet?

Luis

Yeah, he came by to collect as usual.

Frankie

Luis, I told you so many times. You shouldn't pay him. He only keeps
coming back for more. I'll never give that creep another dime as long as
I live. I don't care what he does.

Luis

Yes, but you can keep hiding. I have to be right here—I can't move—this
is where my bread and butter is, and here is where he comes for his.

Papo

Luis, did you tell Frankie about Rosa?

Luis

Oh yes. Frankie, Rosa said to tell you that she went to the doctor. She
left the children with your mother.

Frankie

Is she sick? Is there something wrong?

Luis

I don't think so. She just said that she was going for a checkup. Probably
just making sure the baby's still there. What do you think, Frankie? Will
it be a boy or a girl?

Frankie

Ha ha. What do you think? It will be a girl. This time, it will be my little
princess. A beautiful child—beautiful like her father. A beautiful princess
to charm all you weak, puny men. She will dazzle the world. She will
sing and dance for kings and destroy the minds of all men. She will be

lovely and graceful and witty and filled with love and life. She will tell all the world "I am Gloria Cristo, the daughter of Frankie Cristo, born in the slums of El Barrio and destined to bring light into the world to make you all smile and laugh and dream and believe in tomorrow—a tomorrow without fear or hate or anguish or greed, a tomorrow without garbage and roaches and landlords and cops. Behold my beauty—it is a reflection of your own; see me dance—it is your spirit released from the chains of your bondage of self-despair; listen to my song—it is the music of the riches before you believed in your own weakness and ugliness and poverty.

Luis

Bah! Look at this man. He is mad—dancing in the streets, talking of a princess, of kings. Always talking nonsense.

Frankie

You call my daughter nonsense? You dare to call my princess nonsense? I challenge you to a duel. Come choose your weapon.

Luis

Ave María. The man has lost his senses. Look at him.

Papo

Hey, Frankie. Have you told Murphy about her? Will she dazzle him too? Will she dance for him?

Frankie

Murphy, Murphy? My princess dance for Murphy? Hah hah! That fool. He won't dare set eyes on her. His own greed will turn him to stone if he comes within eyesight of her. Yes, he will turn to stone if he dares bring his ugliness near her beauty, and when he turns to stone I will run out in front of him and shoot craps on his nose . . . ha . . . ha . . .

Then I will build a huge arena out in front of him, right here in the middle of the street and have dozens of cock fights before his very eyes. I will send to Puerto Rico for the finest fighting cocks in the world, and they will parade up and down his back, and the champion cock will perch on his head and crow his victory cu cu rucu . . . cucurucu cucurucu.

Luis

Now we have cock fights. First a princess and a king, now a cockfight. Papo, why do you continue to listen to this fantasy? Go to your children, Frankie. They are waiting for you at your mother's house.

Papo

"No! Hey, Frankie, there's a crap game in the alley. Go get in the action."

Frankie

Action? Ha ha, yeah! I never expected the bank to be open so late. Ha ha, I think I'll go over and make a withdrawal. Yeah, action—ha, ha—see you later. Got to see a man about my kid's scholarship.

(He runs off to the dice game.)

"Hey, baby, make room for the keed! What's the point?"

Voice

Six! Five bucks, he don't score!

Luis

What is he talking about? Scholarship! Little Rubén is only five. I think that man is loco. He babbles like a fool. (Voices in the dice game continue subdued as Rosa enters stage left. She is pregnant.)

Papo

Cool it, Luis. Here comes Rosa.

Rosa

(To Luis) Has Frankie come from work yet?

Luis

Yeah! Oh . . . er yeah . . . er uh . . . he said he had to go get something for the kids.

Papo

Yeah, he said something about greens—lettuce I think it was.

Rosa

Lettuce? Frankie? Buy lettuce?

Luis

Er, ah, he says that he'll be home right away to clean up.

Papo

He's probably cleaning up right now.

Rosa

Now? You mean he already came back?

Papo

Man, that guy comes back every time.

Rosa

What?

Luis

Oh yes, Frankie will be back any time now.

Rosa

Well, I'll go upstairs. It's almost seven.

Papo

With Frankie rolling, it'll be seven all night long.

Rosa

What did you say?—now I know where he is.

(She is cut off by Papo who throws the can of beer over his shoulder toward the alleyway.)

Papo

(Shouting) La hara!

(The dice players break and run in all directions as Murphy the policeman appears. He runs out and disappears into the alleyway.)

Rosa

Oh! That man!
(Rosa exits through the tenement doorway as Murphy reenters through the alleyway; he turns and looks back into the alley as Frankie appears at the

tenement door and peeks out. As Murphy turns, Frankie darts back into the hallway. Murphy looks around suspiciously and then walks out.)

Murphy

(To Luis) I'll be back!

(He exits!)

Frankie

(Entering through the tenement door, counting money and laughing.) Is he gone? Ha ha! Here you are, Papo! (He hands Papo twenty dollars.) Having you around is better than social security. Luis, hold on to this until I am ready to go home.

(He hands his winnings to Luis.) I think I start collecting the night numbers.

(Doña María, a fat, aging lady, waddles in stage left.)

Hello, Doña María, how are you?

Doña María

Oh! Frankie, if you only knew what I have been through! Oh! All week long, I have been so worried. Finally, today I went to see the doctor.

Frankie

Is your rheumatism bothering you again?

Doña María

No, it's just that I was feeling so well lately I was sure something was wrong with me.

(Frankie laughing)

Frankie, what do you like for today, ah?

Frankie

Quien sabe they are all beautiful numbers, right, Papo?

Papo

(counting money) "Four . . . seventy-five."

Doña María

Is that the number you're going to play?

Papo

Eh? No, that's the price of a bottle of rum. See you later.

(Papo exits)

Luis

How are the children, Doña María?

Doña María

As usual, some are well, other not so good.

Frankie

They'll make a great football team someday.

Luis

Yes, and the smallest one will be left for water boy.

Doña María

Oh! You always make fun, even the doctor makes fun. Which reminds me, I want to play a number with a zero.

Frankie

Zero? Zero is a potato!

Doña María

Yes, the doctor says I cannot eat any more potatoes! Oh yes, and a nine.

Luis

Nine? That's an elephant. Did the doctor say you should not eat elephants?

Doña María

No, but he say if I keep eating potatoes, I will begin to look like an elephant.

Frankie

Okay, and since you are a lady, we'll make the last number six. I'll write that down (he writes)—a potato makes an elephant out of a lady.

Doña María

Here you are, Frankie, I only have a quarter.

Frankie

And I too will add a quarter for you and put two dollars for myself. I feel lucky.

Voice

(From off the stage) "Frankie!"

Doña María

I have to go now, Frankie. Luis, can I have two pounds of beans on credit?

Luis

Seguro, come inside. (Both exit into the store.)

Feminine Voice

Frankie. (Frankie turns, facing the building and looks up.)

Frankie

Oh! Hello, Doña Carmen. How are you?

Doña Carmen

Fine, thank you, Frankie. Are you collecting?

Frankie

Yes, what would you like?

Doña Carmen

Seven-fifteen." (She throws a quarter down from the window. Murphy appears on stage left unseen by Frankie.)

Frankie

Seven fifteen, right!

Murphy

Did she say seven fifteen?

Frankie

Yes, she said seven . . . (He turns and comes face to face.) Fifteen . . . er . . . ah, but . . . er . . . she's wrong isn't she? Heh heh, it's only seven o'clock, no? Heh heh.

Murphy

"Don't be funny. I'm talking about the number. Personally, I like nine twenty-four."

Frankie

You would. It means donkey.

Murphy

In the hall! (Murphy shoves Frankie into the tenement doorway, and both men disappear into the house. Their voices can be heard outside.)

Murphy

Okay, wise guy . . . cough up . . . Twenty dollars.

Frankie

What you think this is? Home relief? I ain't got no money.

Murphy

Twenty-five dollars!

Frankie

Look, I don't collect no more. I'm working. Ask Tony. I'm working . . . oww!

Murphy

Okay, chump. I'm gonna let you go this time. But the night track just opened yesterday, and I know you'll be collecting. Next time I see you, I want twenty bucks. Got it?

Frankie

Oww!" (Murphy appears at the door of the tenement, looks around and exits.)

End Scene I

Scene II

(A small apartment. The kitchen and living room area are in a single room. The kitchen table *separates* the two areas. The room is dominated by a large rectangular mirror with a picture of Christ and the Sacred Heart in the center. The window sills and the area of the room near the windows are crowded with an assortment of flower pots, cans and boxes with live plants and flowers, a fish tank and a parakeet cage. Other essentials are a sewing machine, a record player and a record cabinet. Rosa is feeding the parakeet as Frankie enters and slams the door.)

Frankie

Coffee! (Rosa continues feeding the parakeet as Frankie throws his raincoat on the sofa and starts to remove his shirt.) That son of a—

Rosa

Frankie! You're not in the street now!

Frankie

Bah! What a dumb cop. You know what everybody hates? Well, do you? Hey, I asked you a question. Do you know what everybody hates?

Rosa

Frankie Cristo?

Frankie

Don't be so smart . . . no . . . not Frankie Cristo. Everybody hates a dumb cop that's what. (He walks to the mirror.)

Frankie

Look, that cop must be crazy—hey, didn't I ask you for some coffee? What's wrong with you? I walk in here with both shoulders busted, and you just stand there feeding that bird.

Rosa (turning)

Everything is funny to you isn't it? Gambling . . . getting beaten by the police—it's all a big joke.

Frankie

Don't you start now. I don't want to hear it. Just forget it. I can take anything he can dish out. Don't you start.

Rosa

You can take it . . . you can take it—that's all you have to say—you can take it. Look at you . . . my God, look at you.

Frankie

It's okay, baby, it don't hurt.

Rosa

Okay? Okay? How many times is it going to be *okay*? How many? Frankie, you can take it, but I can't! I don't want to.

Frankie

Don't be mad, honey. I'm gonna quit . . . real soon . . . I promise.

Rosa

Promise? This is the only promise you ever kept to me (she pats her stomach) ever since I married you, I've been pregnant in the summer and barefoot in the winter.

Frankie

What are you talking about? How about this? Where you think it all came from, ah? That refrigerator—you remember what it was like without a refrigerator?

Rosa

Yes, I used to have to carry the ice up four flights of stairs.

Frankie

Don't be so smart. (He opens the refrigerator and takes out a steak.) How about this? Once upon a time, there was nothing but rice and beans.

Rosa

I thought you like rice and beans.

Frankie

I do! But not for breakfast. Besides look at that—you got a hi-fi set, a sewing machine and your plants. Ha ha, look at them . . . all over the house. Ha ha, a million plants. Every time I walk in here, I feel like Tarzan . . . aaa ooo aaa! (He shouts and beats his chest.) This is the only house in the world that visitors have to bring machetes and survival kits. Whattaya mean we don't need anything else? We need everything else. We got nothing!

Rosa

Frankie, I don't need much. We don't have to be rich. Suppose I lose you. What about the kids? How will I take care of them? Murphy wouldn't chase you around if you weren't in some kind of trouble all the time. We need you here at home. We don't need you running around getting beaten up every day.

Frankie

Look, I don't want to hear it. You understand? I know what I'm doing. I get enough hell out there on the street every day without having to come in here and get more crap from you.

Rosa

Well you're going to get crap from me. I'm your wife. You can take crap from everyone but me, but when you get all messed up, I'm the one who has to suffer. And the kids have to get the worst of it. Frank, you better decide what's important to you . . . your family or the streets.

Frankie

What? Whattayou mean? Whatta you trying to tell me? You don't like what you got? You trying to tell me something? Like you want to leave? Is that it? So long, Frankie? That what it is?

Rosa

I didn't say that—

Frankie

No, but you meant it. Right? Right? Rosa, you didn't say it, but that's what was coming down right? Bye, Frankie, it was nice while it was nice but it ain't nice no more? Is that what's coming down?

Rosa

That's your decision, Frankie, not mine. We need you here. We need you whole and sound. If we don't have that, what have we got? You think it's funny and you laugh it off, but one day, Murphy's not going to be so easy on you. You're going to get arrested, then what? What about the kids you're always bragging about? What about little Frankie, the first Puerto Rican president. What about little Rubén, the next Roberto Clemente? What about Miss Universe 1989? The princess who's going to dazzle the world and make everyone forget Marisol? What are they going to be doing while Frankie Cristo sits around in Sing Sing for five years, trying to figure out new ways to beat the system? No, Frankie, it's the same thing either way. If I go back to the island with my father, at least I won't be expecting you to come home every night. I won't have to sit up all night waiting, wondering what you're going to look like when you come through the door . . . if you come through the door at all. If you're not going to think about us, I'll have to go on my own and do it. But when I walk out that door, you remember one thing—it was your decision not mine.

(Pause . . . silence.)

Frankie

"Look, man, do you what you gotta do. I got no ball and chain around you. You knew what you were getting when you did the thing. I'm me. Nothing more. I take care of mine the best I can, doing whatever I can and whatever I have to. I ain't gonna let my family go without as long as I can hustle and scuffle to bring home the rice and beans. If you don't like my way, there's nothing I can do to change you . . . you keep talkin' about we don't need anything else . . . about how I got a job . . . ha . . . ha!

Rosa

There you go again. Look at yourself. Everything is a joke!
Honey. We've got two kids already . . . and another one coming.

Frankie

From the size of you, it looks like another dozen.

Rosa

Stop it, Frankie. The boys are getting big. Little Rubén already knows what's going on around him. What am I supposed to tell him if you get arrested? That you're a merchant marine? That you've gone on a trip around the world and won't be back for six months? Or a year? Or five years? Honey, you've got a job. Forget all those crazy schemes of yours. We've got something more beautiful. We've got the kids. We don't need anything else.

Frankie

You call that thing I got 'a job'? Hah, you know what I do there? Ha ha ha. I break things . . . ha ha. All day long, this guy brings me these huge boxes full of things, and I (snap) break them . . . ha ha. Sometimes they don't break, and I gotta throw them on the floor and stomp on them . . . ha ha . . . then there's this guy who works next to me. He breaks things too. All day long, he keeps telling me 'Damn, Frankie, my fingers hurt. I'm going to quit this stupid job.' Or else he says, 'You think I'm stupid? Breaking these things? That godamn foreman is even stupider. He counts the things I break—son of a bitch. This should be his neck (snap) this is his nose (snap) this is his left (snap). No, baby, that ain't no job. Baby, I'm a gambler because that's the only way I know. Everybody gambles on something. Why should there be a law against gambling? Whoever made up that law is crazy. That law is against the law—God's law. It don't say nothing about gambling in the ten commandments. (He turns to the picture of Christ.) He knows that . . . right . . . ain't I right? Talk to me, Daddy . . . see . . . he don't say nothing. You know why? Because he knows . . . ain't that right. I got your number, Daddy. You just look on the scene and don't say nothing because you know that law says I ain't got a chance, that I don't even have the right to dream, that I was born dumb and broke and I gotta stay that way and my kids gotta be that way and their kids gotta be that way. That law says I gotta be satisfied with sixty or seventy bucks a week because I can't read or write good. No, Daddy, they didn't say nothing about a law when they put a rifle in my hand and shipped my butt of to Korea to gamble my life against a million crazy Koreans . . . you know that, don't you, Daddy? Uh-huh, I believe you do. Honey, you see this man? He knows what's happening. (Frankie takes out a bank book and money.) There's nine thousand dollars here, baby. When I make one thousand more, I'm quitting. That should be enough to get Frankie and Rubén through college. I see it this way . . . if I get arrested, the worse I can get is one to five and six months off for good behavior. Hell, baby, Rubén and Frankie are worth six months of my life . . . ain't that right, Daddy? See, he don't say nothing.

Frankie

(Frankie takes dice from his pocket, slowly sinks to his knees before the mirror and rolls the dice on the floor.)

She'll pray in her way, Daddy, and I'll pray in mine 'cause . . . I got your number.

End of Scene II

Scene III

(The scene is set so that the inside of an apartment can be seen, as well as the outside. Tony and Duke are playing cards inside. Murphy comes to the door and knocks.)

Tony

Go see who's there! (Duke goes to the door.)

Duke

It's that cop.

Tony

Which one?

Duke

Murphy.

Tony

Give him five bucks and tell him to beat it. (Duke shoves five dollars out the door and starts to close the door.)

Murphy

I gotta see, Tony.

Duke

He wants to see you.

Tony

All right, let him in. What do you want?

Murphy

The heat's on Tony!

Tony

Look, if you want to discuss the weather, go find somebody else.

Murphy

It's not that. The captain knows there's a lot of action in this block. He wants an arrest.

Tony

An arrest? You crazy. Hey, Duke, listen to this guy. He's satisfied with the pay, but he wants some fringe benefits.

Duke

Whatta you want us to do? Sign a confession?

Tony

Yeah, with small print providing a four-hour day, blue cross and an old-age pension.

Murphy

Look, I'm not kidding. If we don't come up with something, there'll be plain clothes men all over the place.

Tony

What's this *we* stuff? You pregnant or something? If *you* don't come up with an answer, *you're* gonna be all over the place. You better shape up, or you're out of business.

Duke

We could put you *in* business too. Real estate. How would you like to own your own little plot of land? About six feet long, three feet wide and six feet deep?

Murphy

Look, fellas, how about giving me Frankie?

Tony

Frankie? He hasn't been collecting for me regularly since last year. He just started again yesterday.

Duke

Ha ha, not Frankie. I like him. He's funny. Boy, what a way to start back in business too. Ha, some old lady bets a dime on a number and just because she's got twelve kids, he adds two and a half bucks to the bet. Ha, that lucky SOB hit too.

Tony

That's it! Frankie coming to collect on that number. He'll probably have tomorrow's list with him. If you bust him before he gets here, you got your arrest, and we save sixteen hundred dollars.

Murphy

Good! I'll watch for him outside. (Murphy walks toward the door. Frankie enters approaching the door from the outside. As he reaches for it, Murphy opens it but turns to Tony. Frankie runs back out.)

Murphy

No big thing, Tony. Everything will be taken care of. (Murphy nods. Frankie walks by and knocks on door.)

Tony

Come in. (Frankie enters.) What the hell do you want?

(Frankie breaks into laughter and removes his disguise.)

Oh no! Frankie?

Duke

What the hell is that?

Frankie

Ha ha, hey, Duke, you know what everybody hates?

Duke

No, what?

Frankie

Ha ha, a dumb cop. Ha ha, everybody hates a dumb cop . . . ha ha.

Duke

Yeah, ha ha! (Frankie places a list and a pocketful of money on Tony's desk.)

Frankie

Here you are, boss. Good day today. All the old ladies want to send their kids to camp.

Tony

With you around, they'll probably end up owning the camp. Which one's going to hit today?

Frankie

How do I know you're the guy who puts out the number?

Tony

Hell, I believe you sit up all night talking to the horses.

Frankie

(Looking out the window at Murphy) Well, I did have a short conversation with a mule yesterday. (Tony signals Duke to place the list back in Frankie's pocket.)

Say, I'd better collect that money and get out of here. Doña María has already ordered her groceries and hasn't got any money to pay for them.

Tony

(takes money from the desk drawer.) Yeah, here's the money. Count it. (He counts out the money. As Frankie puts the bald head and the moustache, Duke slips the list into Frankie's pocket.)

Frankie

(Counting money) Ya, ha ha . . . I'm over, yeah baby, I made it . . . Dukie. Tony baby, I'm made. You two lousy crooks are my fairy godmother—you're beautiful. Ya, ha ha. (He runs out into the street laughing and bumps into Murphy.) Ya, ha ha . . . halo, officer, ya, ha ha. (He spins around Murphy and runs off. Murphy bewildered watches him run offstage.)

Duke

Ha ha, boy, that Frankie is a funny guy.

Tony

Funny, hell! He's got our money. Get out there and get that cop after him.

(Duke runs out.)

Duke

Hey, Murphy, get that baldy-head guy! That's Frankie.

Murphy

What? (He runs off after Frankie).

End of Scene III

Scene IV

(Doña María and Luis stand in front of the grocery store with shopping bags full of groceries.)

Doña María

Oh, I wish he would hurry. I want to surprise the family for supper.

Luis

He's probably in a dice game somewhere. Why not just take the groceries, and I'll put it on your account?

Doña María

Oh no, I . . . (She is cut off by Frankie who runs from the alleyway, puts the bald head on Luis and the moustache on Doña María. He dances and spins Doña María around, plants a kiss on both her cheeks and carries on excitedly; finally, he stops and bows graciously.)

Frankie

Oh, most beautiful Doña María, royal queen of 109th Street, cesspool of the world. María, mother of a dozen souls, whose beauty is cloaked in the darkness of despair, whose song is muffled by a growling stomach. María, who still prays though God's name is reason, who dreams while the world dares not sleep. María, who gambles against a world that has put nature into a test tube. To you, oh noble queen, I bring great treasures. (He hands her the money.)

Green and white paper—the fuel of the human machine. The high-octane nourishment that has severed the mind from the soul and propelled mankind into a social straightjacket. Be glad that there is little of it for you; for your children will grow to be men as men once were and not as they are now. (He breaks into laughter.) Ha ha ha, you like that, no? I read it in a book and memorized it just for you! Here, Luis . . . and this, hold it for me until I am ready to go home! (Frankie gives money to Luis, who turns and walks into the store as Murphy runs in from the alleyway.)

                    Murphy

Okay, you come here.

                    Frankie

Who, me?

                    Murphy

Yeah! (He takes the list from Frankie's pocket.)

                    Frankie

What's that?

                    Murphy

It's a one-way ticket to Rikers Island.

                    Frankie

Is that anything like Coney Island?

                    Murphy

(Dragging Frankie off) Yeah, it's a boat ride, and sometimes you don't come back for six months or a year or five years.

                    Frankie

(From off stage) Hey, Murphy, you know what Everybody hates?

                  The End

I Got My PhD in Street

I got my PhD in Street
And baby, that's so sweet.
Can't no one beat me at my game,
'cause nothing is more
than ever what I had before.
And I don't need
the glistening treats
that all those cat's are fighting for.
I'm free.
I got my PhD in Street.

I'm way ahead
'cause every way I go
is up
and that's for sure.

Four hundred years
have passed
and I can see
daylight.
I'm here
And I'll kick down
the door
and laugh
Medusa's laugh.
Like me there's more.
No ways
No days
To keep this number
Down.

I got my PhD in Street

My Golden Black

In the middle of nothing she spoke my name
And showed me the darkness of a gray-blue flame
With a fortress of ivory and slivers of gold
Swept in the tumult of a night I sold
To a worldly pattern of voices

My golden black, my golden black
When she goes away, she'll never come back

A vine from a seed I had once sown,
Entwined with a whisper I called my own
It choked off the truth, though the echo remained
The pureness, the beauty was already stained
By my past.

My golden black, my golden black
When she goes away, she'll never come back

She met face to face with a fierce cloud of hate
She smiled all around it and fashioned his fate
Then she watched as I severed a vine from a root
Broke open the shell that surrounded a boot
And looked inside

My golden black, my golden black
When she goes away, she'll never come back

She made a leaf talk, turned a soul inside out
And heard the trees in their autumn shout
"I can do better," to God they screamed
in green, yellow, brown, gold and red
but they dreamed, and we knew it.

My golden black, my golden black
When she goes away she'll never come back

She swallowed a mountain and undressed the sky
While the river of dreams drowned out a sigh
Then we watched a restless *Harlem Night*
As it paced the ground 'neath a bright street light
waiting to happen.

My golden black, my golden black
She went away and never came back

No Orphans for Tía

Cast

Tìa
Rubén
Luis
Lady (Mrs. Saunders)
Papo
Carlos
Gloria
Marshall

Act I
Scene I

(Scene opens with Tía waking the children and going off toward the kitchen. She turns on the radio.)

Tía

Come get up. It's time for school.
(Radio plays while Tía prepares breakfast. Tía maintains dialogue with the radio, agreeing or disagreeing out loud with the announcer's statements.)

(Children yawn and fumble about, and the youngest boy stumbles out of bed.)

Rubén

C'mon, Carlos, you too.

Carlos

Nah! You go first.
(The little one goes off. Carlos rolls over and goes back to sleep. From the kitchen, the old lady calls out.)

Tía

Carlos, Rubén, Gloria, come. Breakfast is almost ready.
(Rubén returns to the bedroom with a wet facecloth and squeezes it over Carlos's back. Carlos leaps up—Rubén runs off.)

Carlos

Yahha! You crazy? Rubén, if I get you—

Rubén

Ha ha! Get up, sleepy.
(Rubén runs off to the next room. Lights go on, and children's screaming and laughter are heard.)

Rubén

Get up all you sleepy heads. *Get up.*

Tía

"Hey, what's going on? Now, get up and wash. You're going to be late. Don't make so much noise."

(Rubén runs into the kitchen.)

Rubén

Tía! Tía! Carlos is hitting me.
(He runs behind her. Carlos stops at the door.)

Carlos

Tía, he put cold water on me. I could catch pneumonia and stuff, and I could die from it. I'm gonna get you (to Rubén).

Tía

Stop this now. Both of you—go get dressed.

Rubén

No, Tía. He's gonna hit me. he told me—see! See! Look at him he did like this.

(He shows fist.)

Tía

A si! Well, I'm going like this to both of you—go! If I hear anymore of this, you won't be going to school—you'll be going to the hospital to unglue Papo's strap from your bottoms. Now go! Where is Gloria? She's worse than you boys. Acaba—breakfast is ready.

RADIO	TIA
En la ciudad de Nueva York. La emisora de la música y las nuevas-al minuto. Otro día de lluvia hoy, terminando en la noche. La temperatura máxima 78 grados, son las 8 menos cuarto de la mañana y aquí tenemos anuncios para la comunidad. Les habla Ramón LaGuerre y brindamos informe sobre oportunidades de trabajo para hoy:	Lluvia? Ave María, idiota—anybody can see the day is clear and sunny. Bah! You are a fool announcing rain without even looking out of the window.
Gran oportunidad para operarias de maquinas—fabricando carteras—todos beneficios—en la fabrica El-Bert—235 oeste de la calle 29—Pregunte por el Señor Morris.	Humph! Operarias! Humph! No les da vergüenza ofreciendo esos trabajos—Every Puerto Rican looking for work in New York will go straight to that job now . . . and they'll only hire one . . . if at all. Cuando aprenderemos?
Otra gran oportunidad. Asistente al Gerente en la compañía de Aseguro-Oneida Insurance Co. of Manhattan.	Now there's a job . . . good job. Who will get it?
Mínimo de seis años de experiencia en la industria commercial y graduación de universidad con bachiler en administración, 156 este de la calle 27, el Señor Delaney a su servicio.	

Mas anuncios sobre
oportunidades mas tarde. Ahora
música—La voz inolvidable de
Manny Román.

(Music)

Gloria

I'm ready! I'm first again. Ow! Tía, Rubén's pulling my hair.

Rubén

I'm first! I was first. She doesn't even have her books anyway. I'm always first. You're always trying to beat me.

Gloria

Tía, somebody took my books. I can't find them.

Tía

Where did you put them?

Gloria

I put them right . . . Rubén, it was you. I know you—you took them.

Rubén

No, Tía—don't, Tía. You know I was here. I didn't do it, Tía. Okay, okay—you always take their side—you always help Gloria . . . never us . . . never me and Carlos. Okay, Tía, okay. I didn't hide her books—I just put them away, so she won't lose them. She's always losing things. No, Tía, don't. I was only trying to help her—no, Tía.

(He runs off.)

Here they are . . . ha ha. You see, Gloria. Tell Tía. Tell her that I was only helping! Tell her!

Tía

All right—basta ya—come all of you. Eat your breakfast, and go before it's late.

(The children sit and eat. Carlos struggles in late.)

Carlos

Gee, Tía, farina again?

Rubén

You don't want it, gi'me. I'll eat it.

Gloria

Put sugar in it, Carlos.

Rubén

Uh-huh! It's good!

Carlos

When we gonna have eggs again, Tía?

Rubén

Mmmm, I like eggs.

Tía

Don't worry, Carlos, we'll have eggs again soon. Eat your farina. It's good for you. It will make you strong.

Rubén

"Maybe Mami will come today, then we will have eggs tomorrow. Right, Tía, Mami brings money sometimes.

Gloria

C'mon, Rubén, finish . . . let's go before it gets late.

Rubén

"Do you think Mami will come, Tía?"

Tía

Maybe . . . come eat up, and brush your teeth. Your Mami is very sick. When she can, she will come. Meantime, eat your farina.

Carlos

Your Mami will bring eggs when she comes—but you won't get any, Rubén, because you have a big mouth and you're always getting people in trouble.

Rubén

Mentira! The eggs will be for me. If you try to get them, I'll sneak up on you at night, and I'll crack one open and splash it in your face. Splash!"

Tía

Enough! Go! You, Gloria, your ears are dirty. Wash them again, and let me see the rest of you . . . hemmmm.
(The children put on their coats, etc., and kiss Tía and depart.)

Children

Bendición, Tía.

Tía

Dios te me bendiga. Be good and don't stay out after school.

(Dissolve)

Scene II

(Scene opens in the bodega. People are making purchases. Tía is in the store. Enter Mrs. Saunders.)

Luis

Yes, madam? Can I help you?

Mrs. Saunders

Yes. I'm trying to locate a lady named Rosa Diaz. I was told she lived in this building, but I can't find her name on the mailbox.

Tía

Listen, Luis, if you think that I'm going to pay twenty-five cents for these little plátanos, you're crazy. You get fifteen cents y va en coche!

Luis

Oh no, Tía, they are very expensive these days.

Tía

Bah! In Puerto Rico, I used to pick them off the trees and sell them for three cents.

Luis

Yes, but that was years ago.

Tía

What? Are you saying that I'm old? I'm not so old that I can't take you over my knee *y darte una nalgada*. Here, give me twenty of them, and don't ask me if I want them delivered. I will carry them myself.

Luis

Whatever you say Tía. I have a delivery for Ramona, your neighbor. Would you like to take it to her?

Tía

Don't get fresh with me now, Luis, and don't think that I can't carry her shopping too, humph!

Luis

Rosa Diaz? Rosa Diaz? Do you know what she looks like?

Tía

Who wants Rosa Diaz?

Luis

What do you want Rosa Diaz for?

Mrs. Saunders

Do you know her?"

Tía

Who are you?

Mrs. Saunders

I'm a social worker from the hospital. I have to see Rosa Diaz. It's about one of our patients.

Tía

What patient?

Mrs. Saunders

I'm sorry, but I'm not free to discuss this matter with anyone. Do you know Mrs. Diaz?

Tía

No. There is no Rosa Diaz around here. You must have the wrong address.

Mrs. Saunders

No, I have it right here. 635 East 111 Street—Rosa Diaz. She is taking care of a little boy by the name of Rubén. Rubén Otero.

Luis

No! Tía is right. There is no one around here by that name. I know all the children in this building, and there is no little boy named Rubén. They moved away.

Tía

Yes! That is right. Now I remember. There was a lady with a little boy. Last year, they moved . . . yes . . . I think they went back to Puerto Rico. Yes . . . I think so . . . a small town . . . in the mountains. I think the name is Columpio . . . something like that. They moved away. Well, Luis, I have to go now. Por favor, Luis, give me meat for the pasteles and put it all on the account. And the plátanos are only fifteen cents—mark it down that way. Let me see . . . humph."

(Camera zooms on Luis's account book. Shows name "Rosa Diaz.")

(Exit Tía.)

Mrs. Saunders

Are you sure? This is very serious. I must find this lady, Mrs. Diaz. It really is very important.

Luis

I am sorry, Miss, but I do not know any Mrs. Diaz. But I'll ask around to the people. Can you tell me what it's about?

Mrs. Saunders

Thank you very much. It's very important. I can't tell you what it's about. But if you find her, have her call me at this number at the hospital.

(Exits)
(Luis waits until the lady leaves. He goes to the back of the store, wakes Papo, and exits.)

Luis

Papo! Take care of the store. I have to go out.

(Dissolve)

Scene III

(Scene reopens at Tía's apartment. Tía is seen entering and preparing to cook. A knock at the door startles her.)

Tía

Who is it?

Luis

It's me, Luis.

(Tía opens the door, and Luis enters.)

Tía, what's wrong? Why did you lie to the lady?

Tía

I did not lie, Luis. I feel something about that lady. What can she want? I haven't seen Rubén's mother for over three years . . . since she gave him to me. She was very sick. She went to Puerto Rico after Francisco was killed in the war. She said I was to keep Rubén until she sent for him or until she came back to New York. She wrote once . . . no . . . twice . . . that's all. That lady is a bad omen. Put her out of your mind. We must forget about her.

Luis

But the lady said something about a patient. Can Isabel be in the hospital? Maybe she is back in New York.

Tía

No se! Isabel never wrote again. Did the lady say anything more about her?

Luis

No. She left right after you did.

Tía

Did she say who she was? What hospital was she from? What did she say?

Luis

Nothing . . . she just asked about you, and she left a phone number . . . hmmm . . . maybe—

Tía

Throw it away—I don't want it. Isabel knows where I am if she needs me.

Luis

No, I was just thinking . . . maybe . . . I thought maybe Paula could help.

Tía

Who? Help what?

Luis

Find out. Maybe Paula could find out who she is and what is going on.

Tía

Paula? Paula who? Quien es Paula? No . . . no . . . I don't want any meddling. Déjalo como se quedó . . . the lady is gone. The less we talk about it, the better. Here, hand me those olives. Bah! She is gone. She will not come back.

Luis

Well, I don't know. Anyway, if anything I can do . . . just call.

Tía

Gracias, Luis. Here, play a number for me with Frankie . . . 420 . . . and tell that man at the barbershop that I will be late with his pasteles.

(Luis exits. Tía continues preparing pasteles, turns on radio, and starts dialogue with commentator. Door opens, and Papo enters with his guitar.)

Papo

Bendición, Ma.

(He walks in. Heads for phonograph and plays record.)

Tía

Don't you bendición me? Where were you all night?

Papo

Ha ha! I was at the barbershop playing in the domino championship of El Barrio.

Tía

I hope it was your guitar that you were playing and not dominoes.

Papo

I played both.

Tía

Mr. Rodriguez was here looking for you. He had work for today and tomorrow. You better take the job. Did you win anything playing dominoes? Or were you your usual self?

Papo

I didn't win, but I played y no me dieron chavo. My partner Quique was drinking too much. He kept ruining my game.

Tía

Of course, you stayed sober all the while.

Papo

Oh, Mami, don't even ask. You know, I always stay in control. Watch me make a four.

(He falls.)

If there's anything I can't stand, it's someone who can't hold his liquor. Me . . . I can drink with any man.

Tía

Yes . . . no doubt you can. Where is the money from yesterday's pasteles?

Papo

Mother, let me tell you . . . listen to this record.

Tía

Papo, don't stall. Dame el dinero.

Papo

Mother, my loving mother . . . listen to this beautiful record.
(The children burst in.)

Gloria

I'm first. I won . . . I won. I beat all of them. I'm home first, Papi.
(The children rush in excitedly and kiss Papo and Tía)

Papo

Come my children, I will sing you a beautiful song of Raphael Hernandez.
Listen . . . oh le lo lai le lo lai . . .

(Lady enters with Rubén.)

Rubén

Papi, Tía, look, a lady came to visit us. She knows Mami.

Papo

A lady . . . an American lady . . . humph. She is pretty. Come in and sit
down. I was about to sing a song of Raphael Hernandez. You will like it.

Mrs. Saunders

You're the lady in the store.

Tía

What do you want?

Papo

(Sings song)

Oh le lo lai . . .

Mrs. Saunders

You are Rosa Diaz? I'm Mrs. Saunders.

Rubén

Tía, she came to the school. She knows you, right? She knows Mami.

Carlos

Come, Rubén, get the maracas. We'll sing with Papi.

Tía

Come, we will talk in the kitchen. You, Gloria, give the children milk.
(Tía and Mrs. Saunders go to the kitchen.)

Mrs. Saunders

Why didn't you tell me you were Rosa Diaz?

Tía

What do you want? Who are you?

Mrs. Saunders

I'm from the hospital. I'm a social worker. Mrs. Otero was a patient.

Tía

Was? Where is she now?

Mrs. Saunders

She was very sick. She stayed in the hospital for six months. She . . .
passed on.

Tía

Ay Dios mío! Ay Dios mío! Ay . . . ay . . . ay.

Papo

Mami . . . qué pasa? Qué pasa?

(He runs into the kitchen.)

Que pasó?

Tía

Nada . . . nada . . . it's okay. Estoy bien . . . Carlos, Gloria, drink your milk, and go out to play. Take Rubén and . . . go.

Gloria

What's the matter, Tía? Are you all right? Do you feel good?

Tía

Just go quickly!

(Children exit.)

Papo

What happened? Who are you anyway? What do you want here with my mother?

Mrs. Saunders

Please, Mrs. Diaz, I'm sorry. Try to compose yourself.

Tía

She was a good person. She suffered so much. Where is she? Can we
see her?

Mrs. Saunders

She has been buried with her husband. It has been several months. Her
body was sent to Puerto Rico.

Tía

I'm sorry I lied to you. I did not know. Thank you for coming to tell us.
Please, you must not tell Rubén . . . Pobrecita Isabel.

Mrs. Saunders

Mrs. Diaz, the reason I'm here . . . well . . . I didn't come just to tell you
of Isabel Otero. I came here to find Rubén.

Tía

Rubén? Rubén? What do you mean to find Rubén?

Mrs. Saunders

I have to see that Rubén is properly taken care of.

Tía

He is. I take care of him. I always take care of him, and I always will take
care of him. You don't need to worry about that. Isabel gave him to me.

Mrs. Saunders

Gave him to you?

Tía

Yes. She gave him to me . . . when she went away . . . to grow up with Carlitos and Gloria.

Papo

Si! She did. She wanted him to be with the children and Tía, my mother, and to learn to sing with Carlos and Gloria . . . for me to teach them. Isabel was like a sister to me.

Mrs. Saunders

Mrs. Diaz, I'm sure you know that I must make a report to the Bureau of Child Welfare.

Tía

What will you report? What will they do? They cannot take away my Rubén from me. What is this report?

Mrs. Saunders

Mrs. Diaz, Rubén is an orphan now. He has no parents. He is officially a ward of the state.

Tía

A what? He is my son . . . my godson. He is my life. He is not an orphan. He is not a ward of the state. You cannot take him. We are his parents. I am his godmother, and my son is his godfather. He is happy here. He has a home . . . a family . . . children. We have raised him since he was a baby.

Mrs. Saunders

Mrs. Diaz, people cannot just give children away. There are laws.

Papo

Laws? What about the baptism? Why can't people give children away? Isabel gave him to us because she could not care for him. Do you think that she did not love him? Do you think that she abandoned him? No! She gave him to my mother because she knew that he would have love here . . . because my mother has been raising children since before you were born. Isabel gave us this child because she knew that Rubén would have here what she herself could not give him. We don't have much . . . but the state cannot give to Rubén in a lifetime what his Tía has given him in the last three years.

Mrs. Saunders

I cannot be the judge of that. I can only send in my report. Please understand—we are only looking out for Rubén's well-being. I will be in touch with you again.

Papo

Wait! You are not going so quickly. You do not think that you have all the information you need.

Tía

Déjala que se vaya . . . she does not care. We do not have to answer to her. She doesn't understand us.

Papo

Wait, Mami . . . she has to know. Rubén is not an orphan. We are his parents when no one else is here. That is what godparents are. We have the baptism certificate from the church.

(He strums guitar and sings.)

Ay le lo lai le lo lai ay le lo lai le lo lai . . . So you see he is our child now anyway . . . ay le lo lai le lo lai . . .

Tía

Recógete, Papo, te está mirando.

Mrs. Saunders

I will be back with some papers for you to fill out and sign.

Tía

No! We will not sign any papers. No! No! Rubén is my godson. That is all your report has to say. La Milagrosa church . . . that is where I baptized him. That is all . . . no papers. Go to the church, they will sign the papers. They will give the report. Now please, I have to finish my pasteles or I do not have food on my table. I have to earn money.

Papo

Ay le lo lai le lo lai, ay le lo lai, lala la ay le lo lai . . . You do not have to go. You may stay . . . but we will talk of other things. I will sing a song of Raphael Hernandez.

Mrs. Saunders

I must go. You will hear from us soon.
(Mrs. Saunders exits. Papo strums guitar and sings.)

(Dissolve)

Scene IV

(Mrs. Saunders, Luis and Paula meet in front of bodega.)

Luis

Thank you for meeting us here. I called you because I want to help in this situation.

Mrs. Saunders

You didn't want to help the other day.

Luis

No. I do—will you let me help?

Mrs. Saunders

How can you help?

Luis

First, I would like to present Paula Rivera. She works in the neighborhood. Can you take a ride with us? We would like to speak to you about Mrs. Diaz . . . and show you something about her you do not know.

(Scene dissolves and reopens in car, driving through the neighborhood.)

Mrs. Saunders

Ms. Rivera, you must understand, Mrs. Diaz is just too old to be looking after a child Rubén's age. And that man, her son, why he was drunk. He just was as drunk as he could be. He could barely stand up. There are other things too. The apartment is too small for so many people, and—

Paula

Wait a minute. Please . . . forgive me for interrupting you, but you're just so out of it. I mean . . . Can't you see . . . I mean look around you. You have a job to do, I know that, but there are so many things that have to be considered. If you really have Rubén's well-being at heart, look around you, Mrs. Saunders. What do you see? I mean besides the garbage cans and the broken cars and the drug addicts. Haven't you ever wondered how people live in this place? I'm sure you have. Do you think you could do it? Do you think you could survive the depression and the dissatisfaction of living in poverty and slums like this? Do you think so? What do you think it takes to bear this burden every day? Think about it, Mrs. Saunders. If you measure things by their endurance of stress, how would you measure personal qualities in the same kind of analysis? And where would you place a person like Tía Rosa on such a scale? Compared, let's say, to the average housewife? Or for that matter, to anybody you know? How many people do you know that can endure this circumstance for so long without relief and hold their heads up high like she does? She's a fantastic old lady—here they come now.

(Luis parks the car.)

Everyday, she makes pasteles and sells them. The children and Papo help her.

(Tía, Papo, and the children emerge from the tenement entrance and disperse up and down the block, carrying shopping bags filled with pasteles. Papo also carries his guitar.)

Mrs. Saunders

Doesn't the father work?

Luis

Papo? Papo is a musician . . . a fine one . . . and a handyman and my assistant at the store . . . and everybody's helper. He's never held a regular job, but he finds his way somehow. Friday and Saturday nights, he plays for a wedding or a dance. The rest of the week, he helps out here and there. Between them, they earn a living and make a lot of people happy. They always pay their bills . . . late but sure. Yes, Papo drinks—like any man and he loves to play dominoes, but he eats like a cancer and he works. He'll never be a bum that's for sure, and look at the children. Do you think they are blind to the garbage, the destitution? No, they're not. They know it's there . . . but they tuck the despair away behind their flashing eyes and laughing faces, and they will grow up with the love and determination only one as hardy as Tía can give them. Put that in your report.

(Papo greets the men in the barbershop, sells pasteles, and strums guitar and sings song. Camera shoots his action while Luis and the lady still converse.)

Mrs. Saunders

What about his wife? Where is she? Why does he live with his mother?

Luis

We won't discuss that. Let's just accept the fact that he raises the children without her.

Paula

Mrs. Saunders, the legal questions involved in Rubén's custody are going to be affected by your report. We brought you here so that we could try to explain some things that you might have judged too quickly with a single visit to Tía's home. You can see that Tía and Papo are taking the place of parents Rubén doesn't have.

Mrs. Saunders

I don't know, Miss. I'm not the person who will judge and rule in this case. I can only report whatever facts I learn. I appreciate your interest in Mrs. Diaz and Rubén, but I'm afraid there's nothing I can do at this point. My report has already been sent in.

(Dissolve)

Scene V

(Paula and Luis enter the bodega. Papo is behind counter.)

Papo

Hola, Luis, cómo sigue el asunto?

Luis

No se decirte, Papo, Paula must speak with Tía to try to work this out—

Papo

Bah! What is there to work out? Why can't that lady mind her business? Everything was fine until that lady came. What do you think, Paula? What will happen?

Paula

I can't be sure, Papo. Let me talk to Tía. I think that you and Tía and the baptism papers will be enough. Do you think a priest will speak up for you?

Papo

A priest? Why a priest? Maybe Tía get one from the church . . . but why? Why isn't it enough that we are his godparents . . . and we have cared for him since he was a baby? Will they take Gloria? Or Carlos? Why only Rubén? They eat the same food . . . live with the same family. Why do they pick on Rubén? We are a family. Families aren't made by law, in a courtroom. They are made by love, in a home. We do not treat Rubén differently because his name is Otero and ours is Diaz. Bah! This country is crazy. In Puerto Rico, there are no orphans. Did you know that? No orphans. Families are big . . . and poor, sometimes. Sometimes the husbands and wives do not stay together, and the names of the children get mixed up in different families . . . but every child has a home . . . donde come uno comen dos . . . where one can eat . . . two can eat.

(Children burst into store. Tía follows.)

Rubén

I'm first! I'm first! Tía! Tía! I won! I won! We sold all our pasteles! Did you sell yours?

Gloria

Papi, I want an ice cream.

Carlos

Me too! C'mon, Papi, get us ice cream. Don Luis, can Papi get out of work now? He has to show us how to play dominoes.

Tía

Humph! Don't you children start bothering your father. He's busy now. Come, get your ice creams and get out. This is not a playground.

Luis

Tía, come here. I want you to meet Paula . . . you know . . . I told you about her.

Paula

Hello, Señora Diaz.

Tía

Paula? Como está, mija? Tu eres PuertoRiqueña? Hmmmm.

Paula

Si, I am.

Tía

Si? I can't tell. You don't have the stain—la mancha del platano.

Luis

Paula thinks she can help.

Tía

Help? Help who?

Rubén

Don Luis, here ten cents for my ice cream.

Carlos, Gloria

Me too! Here. Do you have some bubble gum?

Tía

No bubble gum for you. Get your ice cream—that's all. Go outside and wait for me.

(Children exit.)

Luis

Paula knows about these things. She is in law school and works in the community office.

Tía

Paula, I know you want to help, but I don't know about these things. I will not sign any papers. I will not talk to those people. They will not take my Rubén.

Paula

But we can talk to them. They will understand. You can show them who you are . . . what you are . . . your home—

Tía

No! Why should I show them? What have they ever done for me? I don't even know who they are. They never cared about Rubén before . . . why now?

Paula

It's the law. They just want to make sure Rubén is looked after.

Tía

You don't understand. Let me tell you something—this is not Puerto Rico. These people do not understand us. I saw the way she looked at my pasteles, at Papo, at me. She may never taste my pasteles but she will never like them . . . and she will never understand Papo or anything else.

Papo

Understand me? Hah hah! Everybody understands me. I am the only man everybody understands. I am simple to understand—only my wife does not understand me. I want to be home with my children—teach them to sing and play guitar. I work everyday but don't pay taxes, lunch or carfare, so I end up with just as much as everybody else and no foreman driving me crazy or rush hour people breathing in my face. What is to understand? Don Luis, who else do you trust with your store when you go out?

Tía

Humph, don't brag so much. Get the account—we have to pay Don Luis. Paula, I'm sorry. Rubén is my son. I do not have to prove that or to explain it to anyone. No one will take him from me . . . never! Tell that to the lady.

(Children burst in.)

Come, let's go.

(They all exit.)

End of Scene V.

Scene VI

M.O.S (Paula is seen running out of the courthouse.)

(Dissolve)

Scene VII

(Scene opens in the bodega. Paula enters excitedly.)

Paula

Luis! Luis have you seen Tía or Rubén?

Luis

What happened?

Paula

She's not home! She didn't show up at the court! She could have won the case. I've told her time after time all she had to do is show up . . . even if she didn't sign the papers . . . even without cooperating . . . just being there, ah! Mrs. Saunders *was* going to testify in her favor. This is 1971. The court doesn't just take children like that.

Luis

Did you adjourn again?

Paula

She lost! The judge was . . . oh, what's the use? She could be free of it all now. Why didn't she come when we would have won? She just wouldn't trust me.

Luis

Not you, Paula! It's not you she doesn't trust. It's everybody else—the social worker, the hospital, the lawyers, the courts . . . all those formal, legalistic people. She's never learned to understand them, and they never took time to teach her how. Not you, Paula . . . Them . . . they haven't earned her trust. What about Rubén?

Paula

She must turn him over to them. A Marshall will be here soon.

Luis

She was right! She said it. She said, "If they take Rubén to court they would keep him." Now, she's gone. She won't give him up. How will they find her?

Paula

Where is she? You know where she went—where is she?

Luis

Puerto Rico—remember what she said the first day Mrs. Saunders came? Rosa Diaz moved to Puerto Rico some place called Columpio or something. That is where she must have gone.

Paula

But there's no such place. There's no place in Puerto Rico called Columpio. They'll never find her.

Scene VIII

M.O.S (Shoot scene of Tía and Rubén at airport, boarding a plane.)

(Simultaneous film of marshal climbing tenement stairs, knocking on door.)

Scene IX

Cut to tenement entrance where Papo sits strumming guitar and singing, Carlos and Gloria watch the marshall exit the tenement.

Marshall

Do you know a little boy named Rubén Otero?

Gloria

I'm Rubén Otero.

Carlos

Me, I'm Rubén Otero!

All Together

I'm Rubén Otero, I'm Rubén Otero, I'm Rubén Otero!

Papo

O le lo lai, le lo lai, o le lo lai, le lo lai, etc . . . se fue Pa Columpio, se fue Pa Columpio.

The End

The Tree of It's As If

She was more of a branch
than a tree.
Standing, awaiting her destiny.
We passed
and picked her from the rest,
for no reason
she wasn't the best.
Scraggly, skimpy, and forlorn
on that day she was reborn
as the tree of it's as if.

We dressed her in tinsel
and colorful lights
a Cinderella
of Christmas delights.
She glowed and glimmered
when we were through
And laughed and twinkled
as if she knew
She was the tree of it's as if.

It's as if we belonged
in that little alcove
Sharing a dream
and the magic of love
Living and laughing
as if we were one
savoring each moment
until it was done

It's as if
in our silence
and holding of hands
we derived all the strength
that our living demands
Sharing existence
when we were together
No fantasy this
it was real and forever

It's as if we were home
a man and his wife
Giving each other
the fruits of our life
And our tree was aglow
with the beauty created.
In our rapture
our love consummated

Our tree brought to us
those moments of peace
and though we wished
it would never cease.
We knew deep within
we had to repair
to our separate worlds
with our burdens to bear.
We continued our struggle
with perpetual grief.
Although we were granted
platonic relief
by the tree of it's as if.

The lessons we learned
on that glorious night.
Of the ugly made
Beautiful.
Brought us an insight
To the truth of our lives
and the world
all around us.
We are in it and of it
and should someone doubt us
Ask the tree of it's as if.

Goyo

Goyo was always there. It was probably the only thing one could say about him. Unlike the other bums in the neighborhood, Goyo was . . . well, just . . . there. Gardel, for example, was not an ordinary person, let alone an ordinary bum. Gardel had character. He had a past and a future. He drew attention to himself by simply walking down the street. In fact, that was one of his fundamental characteristics; he was always walking up and down the street. He was not a vagrant who just hung around. He would occasionally stop and comment on something or enter into a conversation with someone, but he was always on the move. No one seemed to know where he was coming from or going to, but he always had a sense of purpose about him. In truth, Gardel should not have been considered a bum, but he was. He was never ill mannered. He was always well dressed: white shirt, tie, jacket, hat, and shined shoes. He always carried a newspaper or notebook. And he was always clean-shaven; his black moustache sharply contrasted against his bright, pink face. He was a real-life version of the actor Adolph Menjou. His cigarettes never touched his lips. Wine bottles did, but cigarettes? Never! These were separated from his mouth by a cigarette holder.

The man was an aristocrat! Bum? Maybe. Aristocrat? Definitely!

He was said to be a poet, a scholar and a member of a wealthy and famous family in Puerto Rico. Such was the legend of this gentleman bum that walked alone through the streets of El Barrio and occasionally drank with Goyo and others.

But Goyo had no legend; that's why Frankie thought of Goyo most of all.

Frankie was standing on the corner of 109th Street and Lexington Avenue, watching the bulldozers shovel up and trucks haul away the rubble that had once been a tenement-lined city block—his block. He was a young man in his early twenties. Although he was in civilian clothes, he leaned on a military duffel bag, crammed to its brim with all his belongings. Four years earlier, as a teenager, he had joined the navy to see the world. Now he was back, and although he had seen some of it, the only part of the world he really knew was being shoveled away before his eyes.

And all he could think of was Goyo. He remembered that Goyo had always been there.

Goyo was a big, burly ugly man who stumbled about the block in filth and stench and whose occasional, guttural, mumbling was incomprehensible. He resembled the character *Bluto*, the large, muscular antagonist in the *Popeye* cartoons. Like Bluto, he had a black, scraggly beard that covered his face. He was never known to trim it, yet it never seemed to grow. Like Goyo himself, it was just . . . there.

Goyo was never seen eating, yet he was a corpulent man. He never begged and had no known income, yet he always managed to have a bottle of wine. The wine was his apparent "raison d'être." It was also the source of his perpetual conflict with Veterano.

Veterano, like Gardel, had something to be said about him. His name told his story. He was a veteran of World War II. He had earned a Purple Heart as a member of the illustrious Sixty-Fifth Infantry Regiment from Puerto Rico. He drank, chain-smoked and swore, cursing randomly or specifically at everything and anything (or anybody), whenever it occurred to him. He was a slight, noisy fellow whose main preoccupation appeared to be heaping abuse on Goyo and stealing Goyo's wine. He, despite his military disability pension, was a beggar as well as a bum in the people's eyes. Goyo was his sounding board. Because Goyo was always there.

Frankie had first become consciously aware of Goyo's existence one evening when performing his daily chores. Frankie, then eight years old, was hauling a garbage pail around the tenement stairwell toward the back alley when he encountered the huge bulk of a man curled up, asleep under the stairs. Frankie's breath caught in his throat. He tiptoed by as fear gripped him. He gasped for breath once he passed through the back door into the narrow alleyway where the trash cans were lined up. His heartbeat quickened, and he thought of Jack climbing the beanstalk and slipping by the sleeping giant.

Having emptied his pail, Frankie stepped stealthily back into the hallway, his eyes seeking the base of the stairs where Goyo slept. It was empty. Frankie leaped frantically past the spot, grabbed the handrail and swung up the steps, timing his stride to jump two steps at a time up the stairway. Suddenly, he found himself being swung into the air, two large, powerful hands gripping him fully around the ribs. His nostrils flared as they filled with the stench of foul breath, and he looked into the grimy, bearded face that sent chills through his body. Goyo grunted and smiled—all yellow teeth. His eyes were shiny, black dots surrounded by grungy whites, traced through with red lines. He set Frankie down on the first landing and, ever so gently, patted the boy on his head without saying a word.

Frankie stood aghast, trembling as he watched the fearful figure trundle away.

Having survived that episode with Goyo, Frankie went about a normal childhood in the adventure-filled El Barrio of New York City. Now and then, when an occasion brought fear to Frankie, he thought about Goyo, smiled and ventured forth to meet his challenges. On those occasions, Frankie would always look around the block to see if Goyo was still around. Goyo was always there.

One day, Veterano was being particularly belligerent, baiting Goyo and making public pronouncements at everyone in general and no one in particular.

"Give me some money," he barked as Frankie walked by. "I need to get some wine!"

Frankie jumped back startled and tripped against a parked car. He didn't fall, but a twenty-five-cent coin fell from his hand, rolling across the sidewalk. Veterano pounced on the coin, laughing gleefully.

"Just what I needed little boy. How nice of you to think of me. Don't worry, just tell your mother that you gave it to Veterano, the man who crossed the seas and almost gave his life so that we could all be free. She'll be glad you were so kind!"

"Give me back my quarter," said Frankie.

"I'll give you nothing—a good smack, maybe." Veterano's laughter was gone now, indignation on his face.

However, his interest in Frankie and the quarter had diverted his attention from Goyo, whose lumbering figure now almost enveloped him. Goyo's massive hand closed around the back of Veterano's neck. Suddenly, the boldness was gone from the squirming little man. Goyo grumbled something, and Frankie saw Veterano's bony hand extended toward him, offering the coin.

Frankie had taken his quarter and thanked Goyo, who laughed through his cracked teeth. Frankie turned and left, feeling an almost imperceptible caress on his head. Behind him, Veterano's voice once more filled the air with profanities.

Returning to the present, Frankie shouldered his duffel bag and crossed Lexington Avenue to the bus stop. The rest of the neighborhood was still pretty much intact. Although Frankie hadn't yet seen a familiar face, the East Side of Lexington Avenue had not been affected by the demolition. The lineup of buildings and storefronts were as he remembered them, and he was sure that many of the same people were still around; while on his side of Lexington Avenue, friends and family were dispersed to the four winds. *Everything changes*, he thought, *and everything stays the same.*

His eyes swept over the demolition site. Again he sought the ever-present Goyo. Seeing only the excavation process, his thoughts returned to his last summer in El Barrio. On a hot, sunny Saturday afternoon, Gardel had turned into 109th Street, going to and coming from somewhere. He stopped to share some conversation with the bums.

Frankie, now in his late teens, had concluded a game of stickball. Together with his friends, he was relaxing on a stoop, drinking a piragua, shaved ice drenched in with coconut juice. Gardel was expansive that day. He sauntered over to the group of boys. Goyo lumbered after him.

"Well, well," Gardel exclaimed, producing his notebook and a pencil.

"Let's see who among you is clever enough to answer this riddle," he asked. He drew a line and inclined the length of the page.

"If this is a hill at a forty-five-degree angle, how long will it take an egg to roll down the hill?"

"Ten minutes," answered one boy.

"A minute."

"One hour."

"Twenty seconds."

"You can't tell," called Frankie. "You haven't given us enough information."

Gardel turned and fixed his gaze on the boy.

"Aha," he said, "here is the clever one. And just what other information must you have to solve the riddle?"

"We gotta know the length of the hill and the speed the egg travels," beamed Frankie, proudly.

"Is that all?" asked Gardel.

Frankie searched his mind. He recoiled as his nostrils filled with a foul odor. Looking up, he saw Goyo scowling and leaning over Gardel, who leaned over Frankie, who leaned over the notebook.

"No, that's not all," continued Frankie, arrogant now, matching wits with the drunken sage. "You have to tell us where the egg is."

"Up," answered Gardel, with a roar of laughter, his cigarette holder waving in the air, "the chicken's ass!"

There was a momentary, stunned silence among the boys before they all broke out laughing. Gardel was now strutting away in his white shoes and white straw Panama hat.

Frankie, chagrined, laughing, in spite of himself, looked up at the ominous hulk called Goyo, laughing hoarsely also, his mouth cavernous and black, minus the yellow teeth Frankie remembered. But the big blunt hand came down tenderly on Frankie's head, patting him softly before moving off clumsily after Gardel.

Today, after four years' absence, watching 109th Street disappear before his eyes, Frankie wondered once more about Goyo. There were other bums that came and went on 109th Street. Frankie didn't purposely keep track of them all, but he speculated occasionally about their survival. *What had they ever aspired to be or do as children?* he wondered. What had they answered to the age-old question adults always asked? And what had become of them during his four years away from home?

Frankie's view of 109th Street was suddenly obstructed as the bus pulled to a stop in front of him and brought him back to the present again. He swung his duffel bag on board and stepped in, searching immediately for a window seat. He dropped in the two coins, took a seat and turned to look once more at the huge hole in the ground that once was his *"turf.* The bus pulled out as Frankie scanned the scene for the last time.

The entire two-block area was fenced in, from 108th Street to 110th Street, from Park Avenue to Lexington Avenue. The trucks, bulldozers and workers entered the grounds through a gate on the far side where Park Avenue crossed 109th Street. By the gate stood a little guard shack. Several men clustered around near the shack. Frankie's eyes riveted on one of the men. In the distance, he was just a big, dark figure clutching the fence, looking into the excavation and swaying from side to side.

The bus swept past 110th Street. His view of the site was now replaced by large, brown tenements, storefronts, pedestrians, and parked cars. Frankie jumped to his feet and started for the door of the bus. Could it be Goyo? The ugly, dirty, unintelligible bum who struck fear in children and revulsion in adults? Who survived the elements and shared his humanity through his fingertips? A gust of wind blew through the open window. Frankie felt the slightest touch of it brush through his hair. He stopped suddenly, traced the course of the wind over his head, smiled and returned to his seat.

No need to go back, he thought. *Goyo was always there.*

Lita Germaine

On a cold and brittle November night
God smiled down with all her might
She picked out a girl with locks of gold
And to her the miracle of life she told.

She mingled together heartache and tears
Spiced it with love, and a smile chased all fears.
While the city below was fast asleep
A baby's shrill cry made the young mother weep.

Hair dark and tawny and soft as a breeze;
Skin soft and golden, like honey from Bee's
So let this memory always remain,
For this was the birthday of Lita Germaine

Puerto Rican Woman

Fountain of LIFE
Inspiration of DREAMS
Tender breath of STRENGTH
That forges endless FAITH
Imbued with PATIENCE
And fosters UNDERSTANDING
With MIND and SPIRIT OF GRACE
That LIGHTS and GUIDES
And LEADS THE WAY

Librarian

Buried,
Seeing sunshine from afar
Illuminating
dirty bricks and windows . . .

Crushed,
Existing in the dimness
of walls and desks
and shelves
and backs of silent people . . .

Engulfed,
By the eternal verities
In overwhelming volumes
From Adam on . . .

Alive,
And warm and vibrant
Exciting eyes
Awaiting
Re-communion with the world
As the sun sinks . . .

The following is an excerpt from the sequel to the novel *"Frankie Cristo"*.

Chapter 1

"I got my greetings, man." Joaquin had raced up five flights of stairs, banged down the door and stood panting and excited in Frankie's tiny bedroom, shaking him awake.

"I got my greetings, man—the United States Army kind of greetings . . . hup, two, three, four . . . them kind of greetings! Welcome to Korea greetings. Happy New Year, come join the thousands of other young men freezing their butts off in an unknown land kind of greetings. Raffle tickets are free. First prize is a bullet up your you know what kind of greetings."

"Oh shit, when do you go? Maybe you'll see Johnny there or my brother, Rene. He's in Korea. I just got a letter from him yesterday. He's freezing his butt out there. He says it's ten degrees below zero. He says he gotta take off his gloves to shoot his weapon, and his fingers freeze to the trigger when he does. He can't put the rifle down because he's stuck to it."

"I ain't goin'!"

"What 'chu talkin' about, dummy. You got your greetings—you gotta go. No ifs, ands or buts. This ain't no party invitation. There ain't no RSVP attached, you know. This a US official draft notice."

"I ain't no soldier either, man. I never shot no rifle, and I ain't marchin' around gettin' shot at on the other side of the world. I ain't lost nothin' in Korea!"

"You ain't lost nothin' in Leavenworth either. But that's where your goin' if you don't go to the army and keep talkin' that crap!"

"No, I ain't. They can't draft me in the army if I already joined the Air Force."

"What the hell're you talkin' about? You haven't gone and joined the Air Force, have you?"

"Not yet, but I can go down there right now and join. Then I can tell the army I never got no letter. What the hell're they gonna do about that? C'mon, Frankie, let's go over to 125th Street. They got a recruiting station there."

The plan Joaquin had devised was to join the Air Force before his reporting date for the army. He reasoned that whatever the enlistment in the Air Force held for him, it did not include trudging around the front lines in the freezing cold of a mine-infested place called Korea that he never even knew existed two years ago. He had never heard the place mentioned in his history or geography classes.

Frankie had never given any thought to the possibility of military service—this, despite the fact that his brother had been drafted less than a year ago and several members of the Saints were already in the military, some drafted, others enlisted, and many serving in Korea as they spoke. He had his mind on sports, Reina and the prospects of finding a job between now and September, when he would enter college. His applications had already been submitted to many local colleges, and he expected to be receiving acceptance letters soon. He agreed to walk over with Joaquin to keep him company and offer moral support while Joaquin went through the rituals and formalities of enlistment.

The recruiting station was nothing more that a street-level storefront with three rows of folding chairs, arranged five per row, auditorium style, facing in from the door on each side of an aisle leading down the middle of the room, from the entrance to the reception desk. Behind the desk sat a crew-cut army sergeant in uniform. Behind him were several cubicles, each with a small desk and chair. The walls were plastered with colorful recruitment posters for every branch of the service.

"Howdy, gents," came the booming voice of the sergeant, as he rose to meet the boys with a square-jawed smile, grey eyes glimmering.

"What'll it be this morning? Ready to head out and get yuh some gooks?" He thrust out his clipboard with a set of forms clamped on it.

"Fill these out and take a seat at one of those desks in the cubicle back there. You'll have an hour to complete the test."

"Not me," said Frankie, "I just walked over to accompany him."

"So what're you gonna do while he takes the test? Just hang around here? Go on, take the test you got nothing to lose. It'll give you a chance to see what it's like whenever your time comes. Give you something to do instead of just hanging around. You're gonna take it one of these days anyway. We can just keep it on file in case you change your mind."

Half an hour later, both Joaquin and Frankie turned in their examination papers to a shocked recruitment sergeant. The scores were identical, even though they had taken the exam in different cubicles. There were no incorrect answers on either one.

"You gotta be shittin' me," exclaimed an equally perplexed army sergeant who emerged from an office at the rear of the recruitment center. "We ain't never had a perfect score in this center. Now we have two."

Chapter 2

Basic training was all about bluster. Hysterical, loud-mouthed drill instructors ranged around the grounds, yelling obscenities and bullying their charges from dawn to dusk. They were filled with the self-righteous conviction that the people who were assigned to them were to be remade into *fighting men* and that this ninety days of brow beating and ballyhoo would accomplish that task.

"You will speak only when spoken to."

"You will address everyone who is senior to you in rank as 'sir'."

"You will recognize who is senior to you in rank as soon as you see them, hear them, smell them or otherwise sense their presence. You will recognize them because they are everyone. Everyone is senior to you because you are no one, nobody, nothing, zero, zilch, nada!"

"Forget everything you ever learned about everything you ever learned."

"There is the right way, the wrong way and *my* way. You will do everything *my* way!"

"You will obey my every command without question. You will eat when I tell you to eat. You will sleep when I tell you to sleep. You will wake when I tell you to wake. You will shit when I tell you to shit. You will not ask 'What color?' because we do not tolerate wise asses!"

"You will wake at 4:00 a.m. Shit, shower, shave and fall out in front of the barracks at 4:30 sharp. Your person, your area and your gear will be spit polished and spotless for inspection at that time. You will not be late."

"I will be your mother, father, sister, and brother. I will not be your girlfriend, so don't try to screw me!"

"Lights out will be at 9:00 p.m. Lights out means all lights. This includes any light you may have in your brain, if you have one—not the light, you fools, a brain. Light's out also means silence. Complete, total and absolute silence. Silence means not a word. Not a sound. Not a move. Not an action. Not a thought. Nothing but sleep!"

"You do not think. You are incapable of thinking. You are not equipped to think. You follow orders. You execute. You do not suggest. You do not invent. You do not create. You do not question. You do what you are told, when you are told, as you are told to do it.

"Is that understood?"

Blank stares was the response.

"I asked you a question. Is that understood?"

"Yes, sir."

"What did you say?"

"Yes, sir." Louder.

"I can't hear you."

"Yes, sir." Louder still.

"I still can't hear you."

"Yers, sir," roared the group.

"Wrong answer," he roared back. "What is the first word out of your mouth?"

"Sir."

"What?"

"Sir, yes, sir."

"Right! Now, is that understood?"

"Sir, yes, sir."

Frankie joined the hysterics. It was a good release of energy and an opportunity to consider and evaluate what was expected of him and how it fit into the mix of all the things he had learned during his short lifetime, much of which was in direct conflict with the ranting of the man who stood before him. As the routine of basic training, or *boot camp* as it was called, became familiar to him, Frankie did his best to fit in. He enjoyed the camaraderie that developed between the recruits and made quick friends among the members. He decided to become *latrine chief*, a job abhorred and avoided by everyone else for obvious reasons. However, Frankie found many advantages to the job. The extra minutes of sleep, the need to be the last one to fall out each morning, (which eventually led to being ignored when missing at roll call) and the measure of supervisory responsibility over the collective hygienic practices of the recruits, together with the exemption from KP and other *shit details*, were more than adequate compensation, in the long term.

After about a month, Frankie stopped falling out for reveille at all. He luxuriated for an extra half hour of sleep, casually strolled to the showers and admonished the last few stragglers to clean up the details of the latrines, reviewing their work before they left. He showered leisurely in solitude for fifteen minutes, dry mopped the floors, gave a quick once-over to the sinks' commodes and mirrors, dressed and, walking carefully in stockinged feet, left the barracks spotless, pulling his brogans on at the front doorsteps. He walked to the front of the line at the mess hall, waving his *special detail* pass and calmly ate breakfast.

Because the time spent in boot camp was primarily about marching, learning the history of the Air Force and shining shoes, Frankie was often reminded of his childhood. Shining shoes was the employment of choice for many of the boys in El Barrio. They got up early, mostly on Saturdays and Sundays, and picked a spot on the corner of a busy avenue, snapping their shine rags to attract attention and customers. Many of the boys had regular customers, a clientele developed over time based on the quality of their service. They were guaranteed a good return for their day's work, every weekend. Several of them had specifically designated spaces that they had claimed by force of consistency and early arrival. They often wrote their names on the pavement and the adjoining walls of the building. Frankie was not among them, although he longed to have a space to earn money—his father would not permit it. "You will not ever," and he emphasized the *ever*, "demean our family name by making a public spectacle of yourself shining other people's shoes," he said sternly. "You may help and you may serve those in need. You may accept their graciousness for it. But you are a Cristo, and you must never be reduced to selling yourself for acts of servility."

He was very persuasive. Frankie never learned to shine shoes.

Faced now with the dilemma of daily inspections and being judged by the quality of the spit-shine of his shoes, Frankie was in a quandary. He did the best he could, but the results were mediocre at best, no matter how hard he tried. So he did the next best thing. Each day, before leaving the barracks in the morning, he switched shoes with Sanabria (the Mirror, they called him), master shoe shiner of the entire outfit. Since Frankie always arrived at the barracks first, he switched the shoes back as he walked in. He never got a *gig*, which represented a negative value for the condition of his shoes.

Sanabria, on the other hand, was often heard ranting and raving around the barracks about the *asshole inspectors*, who were probably so ugly that when they saw themselves in the mirror of his shoes, they just saw a *gig*.

There were other advantages to being *latrine chief* as well. Among them was being able to review everyone else's spaces. As a result, Frankie was able to learn a great deal about each of the members of his unit who had *goodies* and where they were hidden; who had civilian clothes hidden away; who had a camera, a radio, a phonograph and records; who needed what kind of help to keep from *washing out*; and who kept what kind of *stash* of unauthorized items. Such information was invaluable for an entrepreneur. Since there was always a demand for unauthorized goods and since the people who had them kept them secret, Frankie could broker between the person who had the goods and the people who needed or wanted them. The principles of supply and demand were present in this closed society. Frankie Cristo was in business.

There was more. Part of the responsibilities of the Drill Instructor was to ensure that the troops did not become lax during their free time. (what little there was of it) So it was customary for him to stop by the barracks from time to time to check up on the men. These *spot* inspections often turned up unauthorized goods or activities and also gave him an opportunity to learn something about the individual recruits. The recruits, on the other hand, after a few of these events, had designed a system of advance warnings of his coming by stationing a lookout at the head of the stairs and creating a warning system consisting of quick taps on the metal bed frames that were quickly transmitted down the lineup of beds from the front to the back of the barracks, each recruit who heard the taps passing the taps along. The taps would alert the next cubicle of men, who in turn passed the taps along until the last row of beds had been alerted. The rudimentary alert system, however, often broke down when the lookout wasn't doing his job or when radios played too loud or any other minor distraction had the men's attention. On one such occasion, DI Trezise entered the barracks and quickly reached the middle aisle between rows of beds and made his way toward the back before the tapping system could go into effect.

"Attention!" called out a recruit at the front of the barracks, loudly.

The men in the closer cubicles snapped to, but those in the rear were unable to hear the call and continued what they were doing. Trezise moved smartly down the aisle, reaching the last cubicle before the men heard the call. Frankie, Bobby, Washington and Joaquin were busy shining their shoes and telling jokes instead of standing at attention at the head of their beds. They were all laughing aloud at a joke.

"What the hell's so funny?" roared the DI. The group jumped to their feet, dropping shoes, kits, polish and shine cloths and whatever else they had in their hands. Frankie was the last to make it. He had just come down to the top bunk from climbing the rafters to a small door leading to an attic where he kept a cache of goodies. A bag of peanuts slipped from his hands and crashed to the ground in front of him as he landed and came to attention.

"What the hell is all that in the bag, boy?" yelled the DI, his face within an inch of Frankie's.

"Sir, nothing, sir!"

"Nothing? Hell, that *nothing* is scattered all over my clean floors, boy! And it looks like peanuts to me."

"Sir, sorry, sir."

"Sorry, my ass. You'll be the sorriest som'bitch in this barracks if you don't give me a better answer than that."

Joaquin came to the rescue. "Sir, it's a hobby, sir."

Trezise wheeled around to face Joaquin.

"Who the hell's talking to you, boy, and what the hell's peanuts got to do with no damned hobby?"

"Sir, it was part of our lesson today, sir. Our instructor in survival skills said that often something simple, like a hobby could save your life sometimes."

"Boy, you better explain, or your ass is mine!"

"Sir, yes, sir. You see, peanuts are part of a survival technique in the wilderness."

"Wilderness? What the hell you talkin' about, boy? What bullshit story you got about peanuts in the wilderness? You damned smart-ass New Yorkers don't know squat about no wilderness. What kinda hobby you talkin' about? Saturday night shoot-em-ups?"

"Sir, no, sir. We don't do shoot-em-ups. We got us a bird-watching club, sir."

Trezise was now face-to-face with Joaquin, shouting at the top of his lungs.

"A fucking bird-watching club? You two smart-ass New Yorkers spend Saturday night watching birds? Give me a break. You better come up with something better than that. That's it, you got two weeks of KP."

"Sir, it's true, sir," Now it was Frankie's turn to chip in.

"Seriously, sir. We use the peanuts to lure the birds so we can see them, take pictures of them and make a list and find out their eating and living habits. Really sir, really. We named our club after an Indian tribe from right up in this area, right here in upstate New York—the Senecas."

Trezise stared, dumbfounded. He was from upstate New York. He recognized the name of the tribe, and knew that, in fact, the Seneca tribe were the original inhabitants of the area. Frankie pressed on.

"Sir, if the Indians had learned survival in the woods by learning the habits of the birds and the animals of the region, they could hunt for food and make headdresses from their feathers and clothes from the skins. Sir, things like that, sir."

"Oh yeah? So, what's peanuts got to do with that, wise ass? And don't tell me that the Senecas packed salted peanuts for the local raccoons and woodpeckers."

"Sir, no, sir. We were using the peanuts to show just the opposite. How the packaging of the peanuts could be used by the enemy to catch somebody, since it's not natural to the area. Being salted 'n all. The noise of the cellophane wrapper can be heard from a distance, and the English writing on it isn't from Korea or China 'n' stuff like that, sir."

"You know wiseass, I don't believe none of this crap about no bird-watching club, but I'm gonna let this one go by. Now clean up all this crap, and get your butts ready for drill. If I ever find you with any more peanuts or hear any more bullshit about bird-watching on Saturday night in New York City, your ass is grass, and I got the lawn mower. Fall out in ten minutes!"

"Sir, yes, sir."

Trezise left.

The barracks was abuzz with laughter as they got ready for drill. Trezise listened from outside the barracks, himself laughing about the exchange. He knew the magic of such sessions. They were excellent moral builders for the men. It gave them relief from the constant barrage of discipline and the physical and emotional rigors of basic training. The men were becoming a unit, and he was developing affection for them individually and collectively. The camaraderie was probably the most important result of the ninety days called *boot camp*.

Two days later, he surprised them again with an impromptu visit. This time, he caught Frankie climbing the rafters. There were no peanuts or candy in his hands.

"Okay, wise ass, what the hell were you doing up there?" he bellowed.

"Sir, I thought I heard some birds in the attic, sir."

"Birds? Are you fucking nuts or something? Didn't I tell you to stop giving me any more of that bird-watching bullshit?"

"Sir, yes, sir."

"So tell me does your club have a motto?"

"Sir, yes, sir."

"Oh hell, this I gotta hear. What the hell is your motto?"

"Sir, eat my bird, it's only a swallow, sir."

Shocked silence, followed by hysterical, uncontrolled laughter.

The first *weekend pass* that allowed recruits to leave the Base for a civilian visit carried with it a limit of fifty miles radius from the Base. This meant that the men could go to the small town of Geneva or as far away as Rochester or Syracuse. None of this appealed to Frankie, particularly, not in the middle of winter. His sights were set on returning to El Barrio. To do that, he had to get some civilian clothes, money enough to pay for a round-trip, an airfare and the ability to coordinate such a trip without anyone knowing about it, including Joaquin, whose parents would be driving upstate, to the Base, to spend the weekend with Joaquin. Frankie had raised the idea of returning home once but had received such negative reaction from everyone, who were fearful of getting caught and court-martialed, that Frankie never brought it up again. The only person Frankie knew of who had civilian clothes was Joe Gerardi, a college football player who was in the unit but was being recruited for the Base football team and was accorded perks not available to ordinary recruits. Gerardi was a huge man, whose clothes were at least six sizes larger than Frankie's. *A jacket from this source would have to do, large though it may be*, thought Frankie.

One day, when Frankie made the rounds of the barracks, he noticed a civilian shirt that one of the men, named Cardinal, had wrapped around a camera in his *stash*. It was a summer slipover sport shirt, but again, it would have to do. The only problem was that Cardinal moved his camera into his foot locker, by his bunk. The night before the weekend pass, everyone was preparing excitedly for the next day. Frankie crept under his bunk to the adjoining cubicle, where Cardinal sat, shining his shoes. Creeping soundlessly under the bunks, he reached into Cardinal's footlocker, took out the wrapped-up camera, removed the shirt and replaced the camera in the footlocker. Gerardi's jacket was easier. It hung under the military greatcoat, although it was visible from its hiding place, the inspectors never bothered to *gig* Gerardi. He was a valuable commodity to the Base. His size 12 loafers were also displayed under his bunk. Frankie borrowed those as well. He complemented these acquisitions with a pair of his own khaki summer uniform dress pants. The jacket he would wear under his greatcoat. All of the other items he crammed into an overnight carryall bag.

When the Saturday morning bus arrived at 5:30 a.m. to take the recruits with a pass to Geneva, Frankie was among the first on line.

Gerardi's jacket was worn under his greatcoat and could not be seen. Under that, he wore his regular Dress Blues; and under that, a set of long-johns. As soon as the bus arrived at Geneva, Frankie disembarked and walked to the restroom to change clothes, removing his uniform. He slipped into the summer khaki pants and turned up the cuffs; put on his raincoat and tucked it into his pants, providing him with an extra layer and wind-breaking capacity underneath. He pulled the civilian shirt on, over that; and then he put on Gerardi's woolen oversized sport jacket and turned up the collar. He drew a pair of white woolen socks over his regular socks and put on Gerardi's size 12 shoes. He hid his G.I. haircut under Gerardi's baseball cap. The cap swam on his head and covered his eyes. Folding his uniform neatly, he fit it into the carryall. The greatcoat he turned inside out and draped it over his forearm in plain view. Nobody saw it. Or at least, nobody perceived it.

Absurd as he looked, when he stepped out of the rest room, he joined the edge of a group of civilians and blended into the bustle of the bus stop crowd bundled up against the cold.

He was sweating profusely as he negotiated his way past the MPs onto the airport bus and similarly at the airport to the departing plane. Within the hour, he was on a flight to New York City.

They served him a steak for lunch. He was as close to heaven as he ever wished to be.

Once home, he stayed in the small apartment, enjoying the company of his mother and father. Somehow, against his strongest desire to be out and about among his friends and, in particular, to seek out Reina, he resisted. Instead, he reviewed books and letters, sports uniforms, photographs and papers, his basketball, his baseball mitt, his football cleats and all the items that had defined his life until then. He had come to the realization that his life was no longer what it used to be. He had embarked on a journey. He reassured his parents that he would remain close through his letters and that he would pursue his education in the military. By Sunday night, he was back on the bus from Geneva to the Base. No one the wiser, but everyone wondering where he had spent the weekend.

Edwards Brothers Inc.
Blue Ridge Summit, PA. USA
April 13, 2011